THE WOW FACTOR

How Successful Leaders
Manage People & Add Value

Geoff Richmond

THE WOW FACTOR

How Successful Leaders
Manage People & Add Value

Geoff Richmond

Straight Talk

Straight Talk Group books may be ordered through booksellers or by contacting:

Straight Talk Group Pty Ltd.
67 / 155 Brebner Dr,
West Lakes, South Australia 5021
www.straighttalk.com.au
61-(0)8 8239-0122

ISBN: 978-0-6480079-5-1 (hc)
ISBN: 978-0-6480079-7-5 (ebk)

A CiP number for this title can be found at the National Library of Australia.

Cover image © DoctorZed Publishing

Printed in Australia, UK and USA.

Straight Talk Group rev. date 17/05/2017

For Gerry

Dedication

Up until twelve months ago, I would never have expected to be able to put in print something like this. Something, that is, that can never be undone.

This dedication is as special as writing the book itself. Without hesitation, I would like to dedicate this book to the women in my world. My wife, Gerry, has been my rock, supporting me for over forty years and throughout it all enjoying some amazing highs, and equally as devastating lows, but never once doubting me.

My three fabulous daughters, Carrie, Gemma and Libby, have made me proud on so many different levels. They have taken many of the philosophies in this book into their own successful businesses, and by the time this book is launched each of them will have provided us with the special gift—the gift of grandchildren. The count at first draft of this book was two more girls, Charlotte and Marlee, and between first draft and final edit we have been blessed with two grandsons, James and Alfie.

Acknowledgements

Thank you to the people who have supported me through my career. All my employees, in particular my team members (you will understand the difference when you read this book), and of course all the wonderful clients that I have built lifelong relationships with.

I have quoted specific names throughout the book of some people in order to relate stories that better explain the philosophies I have presented. Unfortunately, I have not been able to contact some of the people I wanted to quote and so I have given them fictitious names, Bob and Carol. Although fictitious, their lessons are no less important or significant.

Contents

'There are only three measurements that tell you nearly everything you need to know about your organisation's overall performance: employee engagement, customer satisfaction and cashflow. It goes without saying that no company, small or large, can win over the long run without energised employees who believe in the mission and understand how to achieve it.'

Jack Welch.
Former CEO of GE

Introduction

For many years, even decades, I have held concerns for the way accountants apply their craft. Some may say I have tickets on myself and think I know better than other professionals in my field. Usually it's other accountants, not my clients, nor my staff. They say this because they know I believe the way I assisted clients for over forty years in the accounting profession was the correct and proper way. My humble conviction is that most clients would agree with me. And that's probably all that matters.

This book is the history of what shaped me as an accountant. Like many before me, I made many mistakes and fell into many traps. But, as Nelson Mandela would say, I didn't fail; I either won or I learned. These same mistakes and traps I see others in my profession continue to make in today's ever-changing business climate. Which is why I developed a series of tips and anecdotes to assist any practitioner wishing to improve their accounting practice and, ultimately, their life. Because, what is most important to me and what is at the heart of my 'business-life' philosophy, is this: before you begin to reap the benefits and enjoy the fruits of your own improvements, first make an impact on your clients' lives. What you give you shall receive... and for me it's 'More Time, More Money and More Fun!'

Bear in mind this is my story and the lessons I can impart from it. My philosophies have worked and continue to work for me time in and time out, as they are implemented and utilised. My advice however is simply to see if there's anything in these philosophies you can take away and implement in your own business-life, then establish what works for you and what doesn't. Even if you are entering retirement or in the preceding phase of preparing for retirement, these simple, user-friendly philosophies will, I hope make your business more attractive, more saleable and consequently your retirement more enjoyable. If you are currently in a growth phase of your business, or you have a younger member of your team ready to drive the business, these ideas and philosophies help to give direction for that growth and establish momentum to keep it moving forward.

There's also a chance that you've heard a lot of what I'm about to say before, that what you read in the following pages you might have read somewhere else. That's fine, but as I just mentioned this is my story, my lessons, and that I'm sure you may not have heard before.

Nonetheless, if nothing else, I hope you enjoy the next two hundred pages or so of my 'business-life' story. There are, however, two things I'd like for you to remember:

1. First, the advice given in my tips and anecdotal stories are based on how I did it, how I overcame obstacles and met challenges. They are not necessarily a manual of *how* you should do it too. That's probably a recipe for disaster, but if you take notice and mould your current practice with some of the concepts I'm confident they will make you, your team and your clients happy. The aim is to engage you to *think* and consider the 'what and how' you go about your business-life and compare similar situations to how and what I did. From there you will be able to fine tune things as you deem appropriate.

2. Second, I'm not a journalist. Nor am I a philosopher or doctor. I'm an accountant and business owner. I've therefore written this book from that perspective, nothing else. I've also written it in my conversational language, the way I would say it to you if we were having this discussion face-to-face. So please excuse some of my less than correct grammar and language.

My Blinding Flash of the Obvious (BFO)

Whilst writing this book not so long ago, it dawned on me that a common theme existed with almost every solution, advice or tip I've been conveying to clients and staff for an awfully long time now. It's obvious to me now, but sometimes you don't see the trees from the forest until you step back and take a perspective of the lie of the land. Or you take a helicopter and look at it from above.

Nonetheless I see it now, and it's simply this:

IT'S ALL ABOUT PEOPLE.

You see, being an accountant by trade has shaped my perception to view the world a certain way, to think primarily in numbers.

The reality, as most often is the case, is that the best way to get the result you're after is to focus on relationships: with your team, with your clients, and with your family. If you examine best practice in these areas, the success you are after will naturally follow. Relationships are important to most if not all businesses, therefore businesses should be about relationships.

As Dale Carnegie said in his famous book, *How to Win Friends and Influence People,*[*] 'You can make more friends in two months by becoming genuinely interested in other people than you can in two years by trying to get other people interested in you.'

My Philosophy

As a chartered accountant in my own practice for over thirty-five years, I invariably saw my role as somebody to make a positive impact on my client's lives. Over time, this ultimately developed as my 'business-life philosophy', my modus operandi if you like: More Time, More Money, More Fun!

I'm proud to say that we achieved this with most of our clients over a number of years.

I often noticed that my fellow accountants (and competition) did not have this same M.O., and to be honest this proved to be a good thing for my business. In this respect, most other firms had, and still have today, a contradictory approach to business—less time for their clients, more money for themselves, and let's just all forget about having fun. It seems that these businesses focus solely on their fee structure they have developed or acquired rather than the

---

[*] Dale Carnegie, *How To Win Friends and Influence People*, Simon and Schuster, 2010

clients' needs, wants or desires. That is, the people on the other side of the desk, the humanity behind the numbers.

This 'anti-M.O.' was highlighted when I sold my business and went to work with another firm. In those two years, I discovered how many accounting practices, if they were anything similar to this firm, probably operated. This greatly reinforced my impression of how the majority within the accounting profession treated their clients, and it wasn't a favourable impression. Within months of my arrival, I noticed that a significant number of clients were leaving, never to return. I must admit I was somewhat puzzled in the early days as to why the clients were leaving in droves, but as time went on I realised that the little things that were causing me concern about the new firm were filtering through to clients. Such things as the way they were greeted in reception, the tone of correspondence. It seemed all the 'touchy feely' stuff that make people feel comfortable and at home had disappeared. The new firm didn't know any different but the clients that I had brought over from my previous business certainly did. It turned out they had been spoilt in the past by the way we had treated them: as people, not just a file number or assignment.

I managed to hold the fort together while I stayed, but it wasn't long before I too, like the new firm's clients, decided to look elsewhere. I caught up with one client sometime later to discuss some marketing opportunities when he too explained why he was leaving the new firm. The reason he gave was: 'They aren't proactive.'

I took it on board to mull over later, but if I had asked this client what he meant by not being proactive, I don't believe he would have been able to explain it. It was just a feeling he would've had, a sense that the firm did not engage their client in a way that made him feel welcome, in a way that engaged him as a person and not as a number.

That, essentially, is it in a nutshell: it all comes back to dealing with people.

This client's complaint about lack of proactivity was just a perception, but perception is reality to your clients.

This book will provide many insights into ways to engage the most important people in your practice: your family, your team, and your clients. It's my hope and wish to help accounting practices, such as yours, make a positive impact on the business community and, ultimately, the general community. This can be done by implementing the proven systems I have developed with the help of my team, which are discussed and described throughout this book. I believe these systems will not only vastly improve the offerings made by accountants, but also turbocharge the performance of your business.

A Bit About Geoff Richmond

With nearly forty years in the accounting profession and owning my own business I have seen what works and what doesn't from many angles. At various stages I have been an accountant in my own practice as a sole practitioner and at other times with up to five other partners.

As a sole practitioner, I was able to grow my firm at a rate of 25% per annum for four consecutive years without advertising or purchasing clients. I was able to shape my firm to achieve Key Performance Indicators (KPIs) that gained peer acclaim, even rising to the top quartile of accounting firms in business surveys.[†]

I have developed a deep understanding of the mechanics of business and created concepts to provide value add advice. These concepts typically turn a $5,000 per annum compliance client into a $20,000 to $50,000 per annum consulting client. Furthermore, these clients become advocates and my best referrers of new business.

But don't take it from me, here's what some have to say:

Team Testimonials

'Geoff Richmond, not your typical number cruncher. An entrepreneur and accountant ahead of his time in terms of innovation and a willingness to question our industry's historical norms. Geoff was never satisfied with doing it the 'way we had always done it', he was always looking for ways to improve his business.

'Before 'Value Proposition' became a buzz word, Geoff had already thrown out the time sheets and engaged his clients based on a value pricing model. Geoff was always assessing new software or technology and finding new ways to service his clients. Geoff developed a client education program that started as a monthly breakfast session that later developed into half and full day training programs for his clients. Clients that were better educated about their financials were more engaged and more engaged clients understood the importance of seeking

---

[†] *The Good, the Bad & the Ugly of the Australian Accounting Profession 2014 Report*, Benchmarking Report & Practice Improvement Guide For Australian Accounting Firms, Business Fitness.

advice to make the right decisions. As a result, he became an integral component of his clients' decision making process.

'Rather than simply undertaking a client's regulatory reporting obligations, Geoff's ethos was built around client service. This mindset was built into a whole of office performance standard and enabled his team to have an intimate understanding of his clients' businesses. In turn, this enabled Geoff to achieve a leverage model, enabling professional staff to engage with clients and to provide valued advice in a very efficient manner.'

Chris Stewart—Partner of Commercial & Legal

'When I reflect on my time working for Geoff, I realise how much of an impact his leadership style and business philosophy has had on my professional development. Geoff's emphasis on building a team with a client first mentality, high performance standards and a real engagement with the firm's purpose is unrivalled in my experience. He's always been ahead of the curve in our profession and I expect he will be for years to come.'

Nick Vrees, Fleurieu Accountants

Peer Endorsement

I have known Geoff for over fifteen years having had the pleasure of meeting him at one of our Accountants Bootcamp events in 1999.

As I got to know him better I quickly realised that he is not a person who attends a practice development program, makes some notes, provides lots of positive comments and then does nothing.

He is a classic implementer who has the rare ability to merge his own experience with other ideas that make sense to him and which will work in the environment in which he is operating.

With more than thirty years' public practice experience at a management level, in the capacity of both a sole practitioner and a partner, he is one of the people I frequently talk to when I want some feedback about 'coalface' issues facing firms in todays' environment.

Geoff, better than most in my opinion, really 'gets it' when it comes to organically growing a firm by focusing on value added services to SME's. He's had the courage to step outside the box and try things like trashing time sheets, focusing on SME business development processes, and empowering his team members—many of whom now run their own practices which attests to the value they have placed on his mentorship.

There are only a handful of people who I feel I know well enough to offer a public endorsement as to their integrity and competence. Geoff is certainly one of those people.

If I was starting a practice today, or had an established practice that has hit a brick wall, I would love to have someone like Geoff to help me formulate a growth strategy and hold me accountable for its implementation.

Geoff is a person I hold in the highest regard as a person and a practitioner. He has had amazing experience and I have encouraged him to continue to contribute to the profession in a consulting capacity rather than drifting off into retirement… he has way too much to offer for that!

Sincerely,

Ric Payne

Chairman & CEO, The Principa Group of Companies

~1~

A Fast Track Learning Curve

'Many of life's failures are people who did not realise how close they were to success when they gave up.'

Thomas Edison

My First Job

When I left high school, my fellow graduates had a plan that they wanted me to be involved in. Although nothing so grandly dishonest as a Ponzi scheme or pyramid scam, it was still not something I would be too proud of today. Nonetheless, boys will be boys, and it certainly led me on the path to where I ended up.

My school mates told me to register for unemployment benefits, or the dole as it was known back then, during the school holidays. As far as they were concerned, we'd pick up some easy pocket money while holidaying down at the beach. Unfortunately, within days, as bad luck would have it, the dole office found me a job interview with an accounting firm called Harris & Orchard. I attended the interview with mixed emotions. I was keen to get a job but not just yet. After all, I had some serious partying to do.

Walking through the office doors, I didn't know what to expect. After all, this was my first ever job interview and, unsurprisingly, I was as nervous as I would be arriving on a blind date. I needn't have worried. The staff did their best to put me at ease, and lo and behold, they offered me a job right there and then.

I probably wouldn't even dare do it now, but being young and naïve I had the courage to tell them I couldn't start for a few weeks because I was holidaying with my friends. Could they please delay the start of my employment?

In the big picture, I was extremely lucky that they agreed to delay my start date as I eventually had a very good learning experience there. Sometimes, things just seem to work out for the right reasons.

The holiday at the West Beach Caravan Park was pretty special also! This was the forerunner to how I shaped my career. The three of us had a great time doing things that are probably best left out of this book. Nonetheless, this was the time I set myself up for a career that eventually provided me with some very enjoyable and rewarding outcomes. I do often wonder, however, what experiences I would be writing about if my schoolmates hadn't suggested I registered for the dole or if Harris & Orchard had decided they weren't going to give this young upstart the right to defer my start date. Who knows? I consider myself very lucky with the career path I followed. Yet, like the butterfly effect, if these events didn't fall in to place I could have ended up as a scientist (I had a strong interest in physics and chemistry in my final years of school), a public servant or part of the larger accounting firm environment, all of which I believe would have strangled my development.

As it transpired, Dean Harris and Roger Orchard were wonderful employers who taught me a lot about accounting and a lot about myself. I also met my first business partner Dennis Sims (also a junior who I suspect relished the fact that I had come on board and ensured he was no longer the whipping horse).

Harris & Orchard was the perfect grounding for me. I learnt how an accounting practice should be run in the early 1970s. Dean Harris was a few years older than Roger and had a, let's say, well rounded approach to work and play. Deano, as the younger staff fondly called him by, would quite often arrive back to the office later in the afternoon with a few colleagues he'd been out to lunch with. His entourage would often create a bit of entertainment for the troops. Deano's mates were good fun loving blokes, but after a long lunch they were often prone to engage with us with banter best suited to the football change rooms, oftentimes embarrassing Dean and Roger. At the same time, Dean was an excellent accountant who was held with high esteem not only by clients but also by the team.

Roger Orchard, as the new young gun of the firm, was keen to impress and was also a highly regarded accountant. He had a good social network and was heavily involved in Aussie Rules football, mainly at a coaching level at Sacred Heart Old Scholars (SHOC) Football Club. I recall one particular Monday morning when Roger arrived at the office battered and bruised and feeling very sore and sorry for himself. He might have been the junior partner in the firm, but he was well beyond retirement age for Aussie Rules.

As a young seventeen-year-old, also playing and enjoying the great Australian game, I asked him, 'Mr. Orchard, what were you thinking?'

That at my age I had the effrontery to be so cheeky to my boss, the question was probably less a reflection on my own self-confidence than the warm and embracing environment that Dean and Roger had created in the firm.

Roger and Dean without a doubt had a big bearing on my future. I remember Roger teaching me how to do bank reconciliations and preparing manual financial statements. It seems quite mundane now, but the first time I reconciled a bank account without having to spend hours ticking off bank statements or adding machine paper rolls was like winning an important footy match or tennis tournament.

I also remember Roger complimenting me when I prepared my first set of financial statements with, 'I think you might have finally got there!'

I kept these small steps in mind when dealing with team

members over the years, recognising that they needed to walk before they could run and, probably even more so, that the more experienced accountants could always learn to go a step higher.

Our Computer was a Wall with Pigeonholes

Today in 2016, new graduates would not be able to understand or appreciate the countless hours required reconciling the Work in Progress (WIP) for a practice with two offices and eight chargeable staff back in the 1970s. It was a different world back then. Especially the world of accountancy, where all WIPs were manually entered and reconciled! We didn't have computers as you'd know them today. What we had instead was a wall covered with pigeon holes. Each time sheet entry, manually entered on perforated sheets, was slotted into a specific, labelled pigeon hole after the time had been converted to dollars.

Just to give you an idea of the amount of work involved in this process, consider these steps compared to the entry requirements for a current Practice Management System:

i. Each employee would enter their time sheets onto a pre-printed pad with perforations between each entry, detailing the client name, client code, a description of the work, then how many six-minute units in the second to last column.

ii. Each time sheet entry was then multiplied by the hourly rate to arrive at a dollar value, a process left to juniors like myself and admin staff by senior accountants and partners.

iii. Each week we would summarise the time sheets, allocating the chargeable and non-chargeable times and reconcile.

iv. Admin staff would next add all the team members' weekly sheets and enter the total into a Work in Progress Control Ledger.

v. Next, all perforated sheets were collated and then slotted into a pigeonhole we had for each client in numerical order per their client file number.

vi. Next, each pigeonhole was summarised by pulling all the individual time sheets out and added and entered onto a summary sheet.

vii. Once all the individual pigeonholes were summarised they were totalled to arrive at the total WIP.

viii. If this reconciled with the Control Ledger we could pull the summarised sheets out and allocate them to partners for invoicing. If it didn't, however, we had adding machine tape rolls strewn across the office where one person would read out the summary totals while another ticked off the tape.*

ix. If this still didn't reconcile with the Control Ledger, someone (usually me) would have to go back and trawl through each pigeonhole to check the additions on the summaries.

---

* A process of going through each entry on an adding machine roll and with pen in hand ticking off the numbers as the other person called them out.

x. Once the WIP was reconciled, the partners would provide a summary of what was to be invoiced, what was to be left in WIP and what was to be written off for each pigeonhole.

xi. These summaries of invoicing were then entered into a Debtors Subsidiary Ledger where we would have the Sale and Debtor Balance. In turn, this needed to be reconciled with Debtors Control Ledger.

xii. We then had to go back to each pigeonhole and take the WIP adjustments from invoicing off each client summary and reconcile the total again… more dead trees!

As you can imagine, many trees were sacrificed in this reconciliation process. I apologise for dragging you through that process, but if you are worn out just reading the steps can you imagine the psychological trauma of doing that process over and over again!

Maybe it was a kind of Post-Traumatic Stress Disorder, but I had long pushed this drawn out and excruciating process to the back of my mind for a very long time. Even writing it down gives me the shudders. Nonetheless, I'll now use it as a valuable reminder to anyone who dares complain about entering time sheets in our computer systems!

My Second Job: Working for the Opposition

As a know-it-all nineteen-year-old I thought I could better

myself and my future prospects than continue my employment at Harris & Orchard. I had heard along the accounting grapevine that the Australian Taxation Office (ATO) were paying good money for junior staff like myself and even gave time off for undergraduate study.

The grass is always greener on the other side of the fence, so they say. Sometimes you just have to learn that this might not always be the case. I left Harris & Orchard on or about my second-year anniversary at the firm having won an undergraduate intake position with the ATO in the local Adelaide office.

Not only did it significantly fatten my pay cheque, the new job also gave me something quite unexpected: a thorough insight into how Government departments do not work. This was to become my education in what not to do in business.

It started on Day 1. I walked into my assigned area known as the 'Correspondence Division' shocked to see staff sitting on each other's desks chatting away, coffee mug in hand, gossiping about this or that. Certainly not work. Not one single person was 'bum up, head down'. Over the course of the morning, one or two staff would wander to their desk, others begrudgingly following, to read the incoming correspondence and write an appropriate reply. But no sooner had they sat down at their desk than the tea lady strolled onto the floor and everyone was up and strolling around again.

This was pretty much the daily routine over the next couple of months. My superior at this time prompted me to sit for internal exams in order become eligible for a move into the 'Assessing Team'. It's here where I first became aware of how much I had actually learned at Harris & Orchard.

At this end of the assessing spectrum, I had gained a lot of knowledge and understanding of the tax law around personal tax. To me, it was a breeze. I finished the exam halfway through the allocated three hours and decided to go to the closest pub for the next couple of hours with a couple of other staff who had also finished the exam early. As you can imagine, the supervisors were not terribly impressed when we returned, but because we three had the best scores for the exams they had to turn a blind eye (which, as I was now fully aware, was very common place in the ATO).

As it happened, I didn't even last one full year in this job. The turning point came at a university lecture I was required to attend. I felt quite chuffed with an air of superiority when I mentioned to Dennis Sims, the co-worker I met and worked with at Harris & Orchard, that I had nailed some poor taxpayer that week by disallowing expenses he had claimed. Dennis's response still rings in my ears: 'So you are one of those pricks now, are you?'

My chest rapidly deflated and that one comment was the catalyst that saw me leave the ATO after only eight months in their employment.

It dawned on me that the only stimulation I achieved out of working in the ATO was to have a win against taxpayers. That seemed to be a fairly miserable outlook on life. Sure, the ATO was very clear in its training that our role was to ensure that taxpayers paid the correct amount of tax. In fact, it was made very clear that if a taxpayer made a mistake that would cost them tax it was our duty to correct their return for their benefit. That, however, was about as probable as an ATO officer working overtime and not claiming it back in dollars or time in lieu through flexitime.

The time had certainly come for me to move on. I'd had

enough of bureaucratic malaise. In hindsight, though, this time at the ATO was not wasted. It gave me some valuable insights into what the ATO were looking for and how to deal with the systems within. I knew the game they liked to play when the need arises to call the ATO: what information they had, what information they didn't have, and what was most likely to be scrutinised. Not that this enabled me to ever use this information for ill good but it certainly gave me confidence when clients asked whether a certain claim was too ambitious or not.

My Third Job: The Beginning of Value Add Services

I vividly remember sitting on the lounge room floor one evening at home while my wife was out with her friends, flicking through the newspaper and contemplating my next career move. The scars from Dennis's comment about being an 'ATO prick' were still raw so I decided to see what jobs were being advertised. I had no real qualifications to speak of and had just spent the last eight months bludging at the ATO. The only thing I had learned was how to prepare manual financial statements at Harris & Orchard. Not really the résumé that stands out, does it?

Despite my perceived lack of employability, at the age of twenty-one I won my third job while I was still completing my part-time accountancy degree at the then South Australian Institute of Technology (SAIT), now the University of South Australia (UniSA). This was managing the tax division of a small consultancy business that worked with the service station industry. The firm was called TG Young & Rendell.

I had one employee who reported directly to me and she was probably close to sixty years old (sixty doesn't seem so old these days but to a young man barely out of high school she seemed very much over the hill). I also had a team of about six roaming bookkeepers who prepared monthly reports and advised service station owners on a regular basis. The bookkeepers, all male of varying ages, would regularly approach me for advice as none were accountants and the owner of the business with the accounting qualifications didn't seem to do too much at all.

It seemed ironic that at the age of twenty-one and only halfway through my accounting degree I was the go-to person for a team of eight because I was seen as the 'expert'. Again, I was reminded of my debt of gratitude to Harris & Orchard and the amount of knowledge I had learned in those two years because I somehow managed to pull it off. I even impressed a good number of our clients, some of whom are still friends and clients today.

Upon reflection, my time at TG Young & Rendell was where I began to teach myself to challenge my input for the benefit of the client. Every tax return I prepared I challenged myself with this question: 'How can I do a better job than whoever did it last year?'

Initially, I simply identified that the previous person had overlooked something that was still available to the client to claim on their current tax return. If worthwhile, I would even suggest we apply to amend the previous year's return and get a further refund. The accolades that came from clients and the referrals of friends and colleagues buoyed me to make this a motto I kept and still follow today:

If you make someone else happy, they will tell someone else, and in the end you'll feel pretty good about yourself as well.

I would later realise this also meant a better bottom line for my business. This is a motto I have used in training the hundreds of employees I have mentored and nurtured through their time under my tutelage. Funny, that theme of looking after people is there again, something I had discovered forty years ago when I was just starting out.

I remember one story when I did the tax return for an undercover cop. He was seriously undercover. I interpreted what he said as being involved in infiltrating criminal organisations and he had to be very careful what he said to me. I queried him about what actually went on and whether he had uniform expenses to which he replied he never wore one. I then discovered he would often ruin normal street clothing through fights that erupted while on duty and pointed out, to his delight, that he could claim a tax deduction for the costs of replacing or cleaning such clothing.

He had never been told that before and I increased his refund by a significant amount, not to mention his loyalty to me.

My Own Practice at 23 Years Old

Dennis Sims and I both graduated with a degree in accounting from the SAIT at the end of 1978. Dennis had told me that he was either going to be a partner at Harris & Orchard pretty soon or he was out of there. He soon realised it was going to be the latter and he phoned me to see if I would like to join him in starting up our own firm. I was blown away by the concept, but I was actually enjoying what I was doing at TG Young & Rendell.

It then dawned on me that I was more valuable than what I had previously thought. Dennis wanted me and I was now a qualified accountant, so therefore it made sense to be paid more. The boss at TG Young & Rendell was not known for splashing the cash, but surely he saw the value I brought to the firm. I advised Dennis that if the boss didn't give me a pay rise to $12,000 per annum I would join him.

Luckily for me, the boss declined my request. Within weeks, Dennis and I set about establishing Sims Richmond & Associates. I gave notice two months later and we opened our doors on 1st July 1979. Dennis had agreed with Harris & Orchard to buy some of his key clients and I was going along for the ride.

My early days as a partner in my new firm were spent not as a grand visionary leader but as a general handy man. I tiled our staff room, managing to retain all finger tips while cutting them to shape. I also painted a second-hand fridge we had purchased. I basically made sure everything in the office looked professional while Dennis serviced our clients.

This arrangement, however, couldn't last long. Although I would help him out with some number crunching now and again, it wasn't long before I began to feel like a spare wheel: useful, but rarely used. So, Dennis and I had the chat we needed to have. We decided that I should contact some of my former clients at TG Young & Rendell and reconnect with them. It seemed like a reasonable plan of action. I hadn't had the opportunity to say goodbye when I left, I had built good relationships with a lot of them, and I was sure they would've liked to know where I had gone.

In the two years I had been there, I felt I had made a good impression with my clients. As it turned out, a good number of them decided to follow me to my new firm, and some have even stayed with me until today, over thirty years. Knowing that I had good standing with them reinforced my attitude of driving better results for my clients each and every time I did something for them. Later, I even had a number of the roaming bookkeepers chase me up to make joint ventures with them or even do their tax returns after leaving TG Young & Rendell.

* * *

Although I took pride in being self-motivated, Dennis had a great influence on my career. I'm sure I also had a great influence on his. We were both in our early twenties and had not yet started to make the mistakes that we were destined for, nor yet learned many of the lessons we were to learn.

Being young, though, had its benefits. We certainly knew how to mix pleasure with business. Although they weren't a regular occurrence, when we had a long lunch, usually with a client who was inclined to have a drink, we certainly didn't go back to work immediately after. Well, we often went back to work but not 'to work', possibly for another drink or just to turn off the computer on our desk.

One story I still laugh about involved such a long lunch, about five years after we'd been in business. After Dennis and I had shaken hands with the client and returned to the office, we discovered to our bemusement that all our team had gone for the day. In fact, we couldn't even get into the office; we were locked out.

We still had things to do that needed tidying up before the end of the day, so Dennis came up with a plan. We had moved from our second office in the inner eastern suburb of Rose Park by then, but not too far away, barely five hundred metres around the corner. Dennis remembered that there was a large wooden ladder in the garage at the rear of the old office. 'It might still be there,' he said.

We proceeded around the corner and 'borrowed' the ladder so I could climb through an open window on the first floor of our new building. I didn't know where it opened into, but when I literally fell through the window I somehow ended up in the bathroom sink of the men's toilets.

I shudder to think how that would have looked to the residents of Rose Park, let alone our clients. Given it was a residential neighbourhood we are lucky no-one called the police! When I look back on this episode, however, it seemed to epitomise our 'let's give it a go' attitude to life at this stage. Dennis and I were always thinking of ways to find solutions to unusual problems, thinking outside the square to get the best result from any circumstance for our clients. Although this episode was rather comical, I was, and am today, proud that we would simply do what it took to get the job done.

* * *

As well as looking after our clients the best way we could, we also set about ensuring our team enjoyed some fun times. Back in 1980 there were not many firms of our size who were willing to let all members of the team down tools for the afternoon and drink at the boss's expense. One tradition we started was to have the afternoon off for "the race that stops the nation"—the Melbourne Cup. Clients and even friends who were not clients started to learn that Sims Richmond[†] had a great party on Melbourne Cup Day. Over the years, it just grew bigger and bigger.

The office location we had moved into on the eastern edge of Adelaide also had another unexpected benefit. An old bluestone building on Fullarton Road, Rose Park, had a front lawn on which many social events were held. Oftentimes, chairs and trestle tables were dragged out of storage and the caterers brought in to serve chicken and champagne for the whole afternoon.

Lucky for us, just a few years later, the Grand Prix came to Adelaide. The timing couldn't have been better for our business. Every November, for the last race of the calendar F1 year, we erected scaffolding on the front lawn and watched the likes of Ayrton Senna, Alain Prost, Nigel Mansell, and other greats of the racing world scream past us down the main straight. The client functions we organised around this race did wonders for our PR. Some clients may not remember too clearly the details of any business we discussed at these events, but they certainly knew one thing: we cared about them and their businesses.

Later, in the 90s, we demolished the old mansion to build a new three-storey state of the art office building. We wanted to retain some of the culture we had taken great pains to develop, one that we felt was a fun and engaging relationship with our team and clients. With this in mind, we decided to add a rooftop platform on the new building just

[†] We had by now changed the name from Sims Richmond & Associates to Sims Richmond in the early 80s.

for this once a year event. Unfortunately, the Grand Prix left Adelaide in the early 90s to be hosted by Melbourne, but it was replaced by perhaps an even bigger (at least locally) event, The Clipsal 500. Even today, Supercars roar around the same street circuit and the current occupants of our building still enjoy the entertainment and atmosphere from atop Sims Richmond House.

* * *

While promoting a fun-filled environment for both our team and clients, we always had at the front of our mind the intent of helping our clients' businesses perform at their best. Even in the middle of the most raucous social function, Dennis and I would have some very in-depth discussions with clients about their business. One philosophy we launched right at the beginning in 1979 with great effect was:

No set of financial statements would go out to a client without one of us commenting on the result.

This motto has been informally adopted by many reporting packages such as Xero, Spotlight and Gameplan, and some accounting firms, but it is one of the few tools that worked for us in 1979 and is still equally as valuable today and, I believe, beyond.

Every employee that has ever worked for me has been engaged, prompted, tutored, and motivated to deliver in this regard. In fact, it wasn't until sometime later that I realised how this initial mantra had developed into what I would think of my lasting legacy:

*I always saw my role to make a positive impact on my
clients' lives...More Time, More Money, More Fun.*

When Dennis and I decided the importance of making a
comment on each result we produced, we were determined
that it should also be a comment of value. Nothing so banal
as, 'Your Gross Profit is down,' or 'Expenses are up'. Rather,
we wanted our comment to reflect something much deeper
than this. We saw our role as an advisor, someone to help
our client understand the drivers as to why their gross profit
was down, why their expenses were rising and what could be
done to rectify the negatives.

My role now is to continue to mentor accountants, as I
have for forty years with my employees, and to deliver on
this principle. It's my intent that by delivering on this, the
end result will be for both the clients and the accountants to
reap More Time, More Money and More Fun.

Can Aussie Rules Benefit an Accounting Practice?

While I was studying at university, and even after Dennis
and I started Sims Richmond & Associates, I continued to
play Australian Rules Football. I was a reasonable footballer
at amateur level playing in A1 Grade and winning a Best &
Fairest at my club, St Dominic's Football Club, affection-
ately known as St Doms.

I learned a lot about life, friendship and even business
in this environment. A good number of my current best
mates came from my association with football. But what

did this do for my accounting practice? I continued to play until I was thirty and also rose from committee member to Chairman of the club, even coaching the B-grade side for several years.

This taught me several things I may well not have learned had I not played and been so involved with Aussie Rules:

- Leadership
- Teamwork
- People Skills
- Management Skills
- Determination, and
- (equally as important) FUN!

St Doms[‡] was a respected as a tough football team on the oval, but we were the envy of the other amateur league footy clubs for our social gatherings.

My input into the club over many years led to me being awarded Life Membership, which is one of my proudest moments. It's also great to meet business people these days and reminisce about our playing days and St Doms. It's always remembered as having been something special.

One occasion, around the time when Gerry and I were doing our fair share of supporting the club, might have left me with a record that could have been damaging to my career, especially if the wrong people had taken the wrong attitude. In the 80s, St Doms was also renowned for its fund-raising on the eve of the Adelaide Cup, South Australia's premier horse meet. Many people from unrelated clubs and walks of life came in droves to our fundraiser because it had

---

[‡] Unfortunately, St Doms doesn't exist today, having merged with other clubs and over time lost its unique identity.

a great reputation as a fun afternoon, even the chance to have a few bets on, let's say, 'opportunistic' gaming tables. This was the era before the Adelaide Casino had opened its majestic wooden doors and when poker machines were only available in less than reputable joints on the other side of the state border in Broken Hill. So for many the St Doms' Adelaide Cup event was quite a novel experience.

Gerry and I were more than happy to host the function at our place. We sent out invites and let it be known that the show was open to all who paid the entrance fee. Unfortunately, several of the attendees were undercover police from the Liquor Licensing Division. They contacted their uniformed support troops who were parked around the corner. They arrived in large trucks, formidable and threatening police dogs in tow. In all streets surrounding our property, traffic was blocked off. I honestly believe they had the full intention to confiscate everything we had.

They marched in only to be greeted at the gate by my brother-in-law, Terry, who demanded the entrance fee, until he noticed the uniform. Unimpressed, they stormed over to our garage to confront the illegal gamblers. As it turned out, the only one playing the 10c poker machine was a twelve-year-old boy. I don't think it was the big sting they had expected! Later we heard at our unofficial clubrooms, The Caledonian Hotel, that there was a high roller gambling show on the same night somewhere in Adelaide. The organisers had sent an anonymous tip off to police alerting them to our event as a decoy, which they had figured lessened their chances of being raided. It seemed to have worked.

Gerry and I, however, were charged with occupying a common gaming house and were told this represented a criminal record. Ouch.

Some years later I was in a position where I was required to get a police clearance. This was in order to become registered as a responsible person under the Liquor and Gaming Act of South Australia. I was in a meeting with a senior officer of the Liquor Licensing Commission and it was mentioned there was an issue with my application. I knew exactly what that 'issue' was.

I explained the Adelaide Cup event to which the officer responded that was nothing to be worried about, thankfully. That was a bullet I had dodged and since that day I never took such risks again.

So, my experiences at St Doms certainly shaped who I am today. However, if there had been a stricter interpretation of the breach of the law perhaps I would have been dragged to the bench before the first quarter, to use an Aussie Rules cliché, in my accounting career.

I count myself very lucky.

* * *

In mentoring others under my employment, I have also come to realise how my experience as a football coach has influenced my philosophical outlook. Just as a footy coach has to be aware of how to deal differently with different players (or should I say, 'personalities'?), so too does an employer need to treat their employees differently to get the best out of them.

Although, like a parent, an employer shouldn't have favourites, probably the best employee that came under my stewardship was a young man, Chris Stewart, who I consider one of my proudest accountant progenies. The football coach concept of treating each individual differently was made clear to me in one situation involving Chris. His reaction to a particular employee who would expect the office (and me in particular) to celebrate each and every win with a bottle of Moët still resonates with me. Chris's response was one of exasperation.

'Isn't that what she is getting paid for?' with a few expletives thrown in.'

I reminded Chris of one of the fundamentals of working at 2IC Management: FUN. Unless I could get up in the morning expecting to enjoy my day I had pledged to myself that I would not stay in business. So, we set about making our place of business a fun place for our team and our clients, hence the Moët. When the day came when work wasn't fun anymore, that would be the day I would sell up and move on.

Chris was more than happy to follow this mantra but also had the strong work ethic that challenged the need to constantly get a pat on the back. Interestingly, and maybe this was why he became such a great employee, Chris also came from a sporting club background. He intuitively knew the commitment of team sport. Perhaps because of my own football background, I always had one eye on a potential employee's background in team sports. Invariably, experience showed me that those associated with a team sport melded into our firm more often than those who didn't have the same background.

~2~

Common Mistakes

*'Don't be embarrassed by your failures. Learn
from them and start again.'*

Sir Richard Branson

Mistakes & Traps

Being a business owner is hard.

It's hard to keep your head above water for the first five years as a start-up, when, it's estimated, around 75% of businesses go under. It's hard to maintain a consistent cash-flow stream, the lifeblood of any business. It's hard to find new clients. It's hard to keep your clients. It's hard to find good employees. It's hard to keep good employees. It's hard to find work-life balance.

Don't take me the wrong way, there are great benefits to being a business owner, but it isn't easy street. 'Mistakes, I made a few,' as Frank Sinatra sang, but in the end I did do it my way. And so should anyone starting out and making a go of their own business.

However, maybe you don't need to reinvent the wheel. There are some mistakes and traps, I believe, you can avoid, mistakes I made and which I'd like to bring to your attention so that you don't have to go through what I went through. Later, I will outline some tips and anecdotes on how to address them.

Trap #1: Ignoring Work-Life Balance

Even at a young age I was fully committed and dedicated to making Sims Richmond successful. It was daunting. Dennis and I were entering unchartered waters. Dennis had a solid client base, which was a great foundation, but I needed to roll my sleeves up and do my bit for the business. So I worked long hours and we built our firm on a culture that long hours produced the desired outcomes.

We were moderately successful for a couple of young guys starting out. Our practice grew and everybody from junior staff to partners took it upon themselves to embrace our work ethic and do more than just nine to five.

Then something else happened. Just over two years after Sims Richmond had been established, Gerry and I had our first child, Carrie. Fifteen months after that we had Gemma. Gerry had a huge job on her hands looking after two kids under two years' old. With the hours the business demanded, I wasn't much support. Three years later, we had Libby, which didn't make it much easier for Gerry.

Without going into all the trying times this caused us as a family, there is one big message I would like to put to any young guns starting out. I couldn't be prouder of my wife and three daughters, and they of me, but now having little grandchildren around I realise that the days of your kids growing up can never be retrieved.

So, learn from my biggest lesson and ensure you do your best to build your practice around a work-life balance that is best for you and your family.

Trap #2: Not Treating Your People as a Team

In the early days, I considered my employees simply as a means to earn an extra dollar. By leveraging my services, I gained the ability to earn more money from my staff than actually doing the work myself. I always had a very personal approach to my staff, but in my twenties I still treated them as a commodity, as I suspect many practices still do today.

After attending the Accountants Bootcamp in 1999, organised and run by Results Accountants Systems (RAS), we were encouraged to stop using the term 'staff' and replace it with something I was very familiar with from my time at St Doms: TEAM. This was a turning point for me, an 'aha' moment. So much so, I now have trouble using the term staff except when I'm referring to a business that doesn't have a Team with a capital 'T'.

Like the young Geoff Richmond, however, unless you have your 'Team' working together to drive your business in the direction you want it to go, you will undoubtedly encounter problems, as I did over the years. To have your Team all on board, though, they need to be educated and constantly reminded of several key things:

1. The direction you want to drive the business.
2. Be kept up to date with where you and the business are at.
3. What's next.
4. Involve, or at least feel as though they have helped, with mapping out the route the business is taking.
5. Last, but not least, look forward to and enjoy the ride.

With these elements, you will have your whole team on the same bus.

Trap #3: Thinking of Clients as a Fee

Everyone in business wants more clients and everyone wants to keep them as long as possible. In my early days, I considered clients nothing more than a fee. My attitude changed when I realised the importance of building a relationship not a client.

As far as I'm concerned, there are two basic mindsets to building your business. The first is focussed on winning a new client and maximising what fee you can build up to. The second is winning a new client and maximising how much you can improve their life through your expertise. I learned that if you have the second attitude you were, in most cases, going to reap the financial rewards. Once you help your client you get helped in return. It's a simple case of reaping what you sow.

When I was starting out, I, like a lot of practitioners, had the attitude that I knew what was best for the client. Call it the arrogance of youth, but ultimately it meant my way or the highway. I look back with a degree of embarrassment about the way I handled several of my early clients. Notwithstanding the awkwardness of my attitude, I would in fact be much better off financially if I hadn't been so stubborn.

One of the not so smartest things I did happened before I discovered the virtues of fixed pricing. A long-standing client had referred a new client to us, a new but well respected partnership of Pastry Chefs. They were highly qualified and experienced pastry chefs who had made the brave decision to quit their secure jobs and join forces to start their own business. Since then, they have grown to be household names in Adelaide.

We set about preparing a first set of financial statements but the client was slightly miffed by our fee. They approached us to give them a fixed price for the next set of financials. I can't remember the exact details, but I know we were worried about the quality of their bookkeeping and some of the changes in their business that had occurred during the year.

My office manager told them we were unable to quote them a fixed price, using the old chestnut, 'How long is a piece of string?' We didn't know how long it would take to prepare their financials, so how could we quote?

The client, however, was quite persistent. My manager then approached me to resolve the issue. I went to great lengths to draft a detailed letter to make our position more understandable to the client. The letter, however, went the way of the Titanic, a complete disaster. We lost the client after they complained to the client who had referred them and we eventually lost that client as well, to a former employee as it happened (after their restraint agreement had expired, of course).

Like so many accountants and professionals who can't see the trees from the forest, I considered myself justified and right. My stubbornness on charging by the hour blinded me to the way I was treating this client, and how they ultimately felt, belittled.

I have learned a lot since then. This episode was a lesson in humility. It taught me the value, and I guess need, for client engagement over and above client loyalty, which is also more important than client attraction (Chapter 4 sets out the strategies I, together with my team, were able to instigate to engage our clients).

Trap #4: I Only Have Time to Sell

All we have is time to sell!

I often quoted this to clients until I understood the difference between time and value, that clients don't buy time, they buy value. I also made the mistake of thinking the more hours I and my team worked, the better the results we would achieve.

One of my earliest interstate seminars at New England University brought this issue of time and value to light. The lecturer was Keith Cleland, a pioneer in KPIs and Efficiency Analysis, both concepts I constantly use today. One story Keith told, which you may have heard, stands in my memory, the story about an overworked lumberjack. This lumberjack worked the whole day chopping trees without a break but was continually outperformed by the lumberjack next to him who worked less hours but took regular breaks to sharpen his axe. Simple, but a story I have never forgotten.

My attitude changed almost overnight. From feeling guilty if I wasn't the last to leave the office and switch off the lights and air-conditioning, to questioning team members why they were working back late. It's well known that performance levels drop as we get tired, so why do so many professional firms, accountants and lawyers in particular, build their business models around key individuals working ten, twelve, even longer hours every day?

More recently, I attended a seminar in which a speaker highlighted one of the common mistakes of accounting firms, budgeting with resources below their expected target outcomes (or fees). All firms know or can estimate with a degree of accuracy what production they can expect from each employee, what downtime to budget for training, in-house work and just general inefficiencies. To budget for less team members than expected work can have a number of consequences, all of which are bad.

Firstly, and I would suggest most importantly, you will under service your clients. The outcome, however, could correct itself because by under servicing clients some could leave, which means eventually you will have enough resources.

Secondly, by under resourcing you are putting work pressure on someone to over perform or, more likely, a number of people. This is the attitude that says, 'That's OK, we'll just get everyone to work a bit harder (read longer).'

From here more problems arise. In all likelihood, the productivity you allowed for each team member was based on what they did last year while already working excessive hours, which means they will have to work even longer hours to service client's needs. You'll discover sooner or later the consequences of your budgeting when one of your key people explodes at your inquiry to the progress of a job. Worse, when they ask if you've got a minute and they walk into your office with a resignation letter in their hand. So the real issue, and the risk you take, is that the team will get fed up and they'll find greener pastures, leaving you even further behind in production.

When Dennis and I established Sims Richmond & Associates we created a spreadsheet for every year setting out expected fees from current clients and what we expected to win as new work in the coming year. We then allocated numbers to all members of our team to determine what re-source gap we had and then set about finding the required employees to exceed our goals.

I did this in 1979 and continued right up until I sold my practice in 2011. To do otherwise, is to make your business vulnerable to the constant pressures from clients, team, ATO, and even the banks and other institutions relying on regular reports for your clients.

Trap #5: Profit is Derived from Extra Time

How many hours of work can this client create for me?

This mantra was a constant driving force when I first started out, even for quite a few years later. I can remember clearly time and again how I would calculate the sums in my head as I met with the client for the first time. *They have two trading entities, an investment trust, a superfund and a couple of individuals that's got to be at least $X per annum.* Then, once I received their financial statements from their previous accountant, I would head straight to the expenses list and see what they had paid in accounting fees.

For me, profit was a derivative of a simple equation: *Hours x Hourly Rate = Profit*

As I grew older and wiser, I began to see things differently. No longer was profit directly related to hours of work, it was a product of something else, something much more valuable: the success or benefits I brought to my clients.

Once I understood this connection, things improved markedly for both my clients and my business. It was a true win-win situation. My initial meetings with clients then began to change to reflect this new outlook. I began to ask lots of questions about their business, what was working, what wasn't, and even drill down to impress on them how I could be of real help and value to their business.[§]

Trap #6: Letting Growth Kill Your Cashflow

In the early years of Sims Richmond, we experienced a steady and sustainable rate of growth. With every new client we won, our WIP and debtors went up. Our bankers loved us because so did our overdraft.

Dennis and I had been educated by the age-old philosophy of only charging by the hour and only invoicing once the job was completed. This belief was ingrained in our heads. If we did it any other way we'd lose clients.

How wrong I was, and how wrong practices still are today that still think this way. The truth, I discovered much later, is that clients actually hate this model. They never wanted to get their tax returns done in the first place; the ATO forced them to. They then get a tax bill from the ATO and, often at the very same time, they get a whopping bill from the accountant. From an outsider's point of view, other than the fact the ATO forces your client to come back every year for a tax return, it's not a very good business model!

The other downside is that you need a debt collection department or person. Who enjoys chasing clients for

[§] In Chapter 10, *Initial Interview*, I outline the style that I developed to help clients from the outset.

money? How does your relationship with your client feel after you have set the office debt collector on to them? Worse, you have to call and try and extract the dollars yourself?

When I previously operated under this system and I was forced to call the client, two possible scenarios played out. Either I really liked the client, enjoyed their work, enjoyed their company, and I was really worried about upsetting them, or I resented the fact they were having a lovely life-style, eating at the best restaurants, having expensive holidays and so forth, and yet they hadn't paid my fees for over twelve months (I actually never left it this long but I know plenty of accountants who still do).

So, what's the likely outcome? The first client gets treated with kid gloves and the fee I had already discounted because I didn't want to upset them gets discounted again to ensure it gets paid by the end of the month. The second client gets my full rage, and he cops the full force of it when I call. At best, they agree to pay over a few months, but we clearly don't get on and at worse they leave and I have to send my debt collectors after them.

All in all, it's clear this system doesn't work if clients want to live by the adage 'the accountants are last to get paid'.

Trap #7: Diluting Practice Value through Lockup

The previous mistake highlighted the flaws of time billing after the job is completed and in Chapter 6 we discuss how a better model to improve cashflow in your business.

The other factor relevant to the new landscape is the effect this will have on the value of your practice. I don't profess to have negotiated a benefit for myself in this regard, but on reflection it is logical that proper management of lockup will have a significant impact on practice valuations and certainly have a big influence on the mindset of a potential purchaser.[5]

The traditional method of valuing practices on a dollar fee basis is disappearing and purchasers are looking for a return on their investment (ROI). If they are not investing in lockup, they will either be keener to invest or alternatively pay a higher price.

Trap #8: Treating Your People Like Mushrooms

How much should any employee know about the results of the business?

In my years at Sims Richmond, Dennis and I kept business related information close to our chest. Our employees would not have known whether we made a profit, at what rate we were growing or whether we were satisfied with the financial achievements we were achieving. I have discussed the value of my team and admit that in early days I respected all my employees. Nonetheless, my support team were seen more as necessary expenses than valuable contributors to the business.

One of the big mistakes I made, however, was to treat most of our employees like mushrooms: keep them in the

---

[5] This is explained in detail in Chapter 7, *The Effect on the Valuation of your Practice.*

dark and feed them BS. This had the ultimate effect of undermining their trust. I am sure we lost good, honest employees due to our deliberate withholding of where we were heading and what part they would play in that journey.

In fact, we did have two key employees who left our business, both to Dennis' and my absolute shock. We were so keen to keep these employees on a long-term basis that we offered them incentives above market for their level of experience and skills on the proviso they agreed to stay for at least two years. The first shock was when they refused the incentive package. The second shock was when they both left within twelve months of these discussions. On reflection, we never engaged them and listened to what they really wanted in the job; we just tried to buy their loyalty. Later in my career, I realised that you can achieve much more loyalty by making your team feel part of the journey and keeping them aware of how things are going with all aspects of the business.

Because if key employees don't know the results the firm is achieving, or even under-achieving, if they don't even know what the KPIs for the firm are, they don't know where they are. They have no means by which they can compare with other staff, with themselves, and with competing firms. By what other means can they know if they are a top performer or just meandering down the middle of the road? Employees will also be much more engaged if they can celebrate good results and know when to pitch in if things are off track.

Everyone in business will have their own model on how they want to shape their business, and quite rightly so. Without your own personality shining through into your business you will not engage with your clients and your team. However, the mistake is to lose sight of the need to manage every employee's expectations. For the sake of them, and your business, they need to be kept informed.

Trap #9: Getting Bogged in Admin

One of the mistakes we made at Sims Richmond was to keep a tight control of the information that employees were allowed to receive about the financial results of the business. The flow-on effect was that partners in the firm were not involved with business decisions but were instead shunted a lot of mundane administrative work.

Bigger practices employ office managers or PAs to share some of the load, but even then highly qualified people are bogged down with tasks that amount to not much more than filing. At Sims Richmond & Associates, I spent countless hours poring over our practice financials, staying back well into the night on some occasions just to balance our own books. Often I would have to put the file down to attend a client's need, which meant I would then have to find time, usually weeks later, to pick up the file and work out where I was up to. Then, just when I'd get close to resolving it, a client crisis would occur and down our file would go again for a week or two. You can imagine my reaction when Dennis enquired as to how our figures were going?

I didn't like having to do these lower skilled tasks. I also preferred my main fee earners to not get bogged down in admin as well. By implementing systems later, we were able to move the pressure from the key earners to the support team. This had the benefit of making our dealings with clients more refined.

Systems also help manage client expectations, which is one of the keys to building client engagement.

Trap #10: Compliance Practices are Dying

I have serious doubts how a typical compliance model will last for much longer.

Don't get me wrong, I'm not saying compliance is dead. I firmly believe it will be here longer than I will, but I don't know who will make a living solely supplying compliance services. I'm sure there will be innovators who tweak the model and utilise the efficiencies available from current technology. However, those efficiencies translate into the need for less people. If leaders of accounting firms can harness the efficiencies of technology and provide compliance services based on processes, they will free up resources and position their firm to provide additional knowledge-based services and solution driven outcomes. We can predict that modern cloud-based accounting systems like Xero or MYOB will make the processes of preparing statutory financial statements less time consuming and more efficient, therefore in the not too distant future accountants will have more time to offer more services to their clients.

As I said, I don't believe compliance work will disappear entirely, but just as national franchises like H&R Block and ITP have removed personal tax returns from the traditional role of accountants, technology will ultimately drive a number of firms to reduce their fees and try and compete on price.

Trap #11: All Clients are Equal

Unfortunately, there are people out there who we don't enjoy working with. It's normal. We can't always get along with everyone, and I can name a number over the years (but I won't) that I wished we hadn't taken on as clients. Like many accountants, I looked for clients that would generate enough work to keep me and my team busy, and that was usually the only selection criteria.

There were many times during the initial interview when the prospect made some comment that made me cringe, whether it was something unethical or just didn't sit right with my morals. Over time I learned that these types of clients usually let you down, either by not paying when they should, or they were constantly complaining and caused your team to complain to you.

It's a very difficult position when a client has been with you a few years, who also represents a significant income source to the firm and a team member comes to you crying because of the abuse they have just received from the client. I recall having to call a particular client and give them a terse 'please explain your behaviour'. I was very annoyed with how they had treated my staff, and I became quite forthright with them, saying: 'If you can't treat my employees with the respect we give you, we won't be working together anymore. If you have a problem you want to vent, direct it to me and me only!'

It's probably best not to let it get that far and instead have clear client selection criteria.

Trap #12: Too Afraid to Bill the Appropriate Fee

Before I implemented fixed price billing, I always had the fear of raising the invoice after the job was done.

Many times I decided to write off some of the WIP when raising an invoice that was up 20% or more on the previous year. On more than one occasion I received a fee challenge, which often resulted in a further discount. The client was unaware that I had already knocked 10% off the WIP for their job, even though the work justified the full WIP charge. All they saw was the increase on the previous year.

This was always a frustrating time, especially as an accountant who was proud of the service they gave their client. Because WIP represented dollars, which represented money, it feels like setting fire to $50 notes whenever you write off any amount of WIP.

I learned, however, that by starting with a fixed fee based on the previous year's work, it was easy to justify the fee change based on the different circumstances of the current year's work. Even if changes arise after the fixed fee has been agreed, it's easier to negotiate the increase if the client already has a payment plan for the fixed fee arrangement because they are now focused on just the increase rather than the whole fee.

One of our early fixed fee negotiations for a one-off assignment highlights this point. Allan was a client that earned his stripes in the crash repair industry in the 60s and 70s. This was a tough industry where negotiating deals was the difference between sinking and swimming. Allan swam, so he was certainly a tough negotiator.

We had a one-off project for Allan of considerable value that we decided was worth at least $10,000. I first discussed with my team how we were going to put this to Allan and we thought it was probably worth adding a premium that he could beat us down from, say $12,000 to the amount we were after.

In the end, I called Allan and said, 'Allan, we have been discussing the fee for this assignment and we wanted to charge you $10,000. We also know that you always like a challenge of negotiating a deal, so we decided we needed to ask for $12,000 to get what we were hoping for.'

I actually confessed to Allan about our plan to ask for $12,000, expecting him to agree to $10,000. I hoped that this would be fine and we would all be happy. I was wrong.

'What about we agree on $11,000?'

Wow did that feel good at the time! I must have told a thousand people this story.

~3~

TEAM

'The most important thing in communication is hearing what isn't said.'

Peter Drucker

Vision

In 1999 I attended an 'Accountants Bootcamp', my first exposure to two of my biggest mentors, Paul Dunn and Ric Payne. They headed up a group called Results Accountants Systems (RAS), which later morphed into RANONE. Later, Ric branched away to form Principa Alliance.

At the time, RAS was the type of organisation I was looking for to round off the philosophies Dennis and I had already started at Sims Richmond. In fact, a former partner of ours was also at the boot camp and commented to me on Day 1, 'Geoff this is just a lot of what you and Dennis taught us back at Sims Richmond.'

One of the biggest BFOs I took away from this boot camp was the concept of 'Vision'. I had recently parted company with Dennis Sims to form a new firm, 2IC Management, with the intention of being a small boutique firm. I retained one employee, my manager from Sims Richmond (as it had become known), and we worked out of the offices of Sims Richmond utilising their support team and some of their accountants to help my manager with the compliance work.

Immediately on return from the Accountants Bootcamp, I kept my new team involved and informed of what 2IC Management was up to, where we had come from, and where we intended going. In fact, I actively engaged my team to help write the future of the business. This is how I put it to them:

Would you prefer to work in?

1. Firm 1: An organisation that just told you what

to do day in day out and never gave you any explanation as to why? or

2. Firm 2: One where you knew what everybody was aiming to achieve and had an input into how you were going to get there?

I could virtually guarantee which firm would get the best out of their team. Firm 2, of course, because they were part of the cause.

Together we created our vision of the business. Of course, I had an idea of what I wanted my business to look like, but I invited the team to contribute towards what they thought would work and their contribution definitely added to the way 2IC Management evolved. I learned the buy in is always better when a team member is following something they helped create.

Mistakes with the Team

As I mentioned in Trap #8 in Chapter 2, in the early days of Sims Richmond & Associates Dennis and I would develop plans to do one thing or another with the business but never share the ideas or vision with our staff. We had a deep-seated attitude to 'keep them in the dark', thinking, quite wrongly, that it had nothing to do with them. They were 'just staff', after all.

Fortunately, over the years I learned that this attitude only sows the seeds for a potentially a big downfall. Just as fortunate, I also learned that the opposite attitude—a more inclusive and embracing attitude—works so much better for everyone involved in a business, including owners and partners. After selling 2IC Management in 2011, I had the unfortunate experience of working in a firm that knew nothing of inclusivity. You could say they were experts in how to do things wrong. I became part of the team but was also invited and privy to senior management ideas and strategies. This firm were strong adherents of the adage that Dennis and I had once subscribed to of 'keeping them in the dark'.

The problem is, when you treat your staff with such a dismissive attitude, they do not become team players. The result is a deteriorating work ethic and dysfunctional departments. Gossip starts. Blatant disregard for due processes creeps in. Disrespect grows like weeds in the office. The 'Us Vs Them' attitude of decision makers filters down to staff and they begin to have constant chats in the lunch room and at the watercooler about what you may or may not be up to. Sometimes this can build unrest from misconceived uncertainty. At worst, it effects the bottom line of the business.

Not long after I began my new role in the business, I distinctly remember one of the receptionists commenting on something that appalled me: 'That's another client lost.'

This was her perception on something she had heard or witnessed. Thankfully, as it turned out, the client she was referring to was one of the firm's largest clients and she was totally wrong. But what it highlighted was the negative atmosphere that pervaded through each corridor of the business. The energy this drains from the organisation is so damaging, and it eventually gets to the stage where individuals either begin looking for the latest bit of negative gossip about a colleague or boss, or they start scanning employment websites for job vacancies at other firms.

The proof was in the pudding at this firm where they had approximately 100% turnover of employees in a two-year period, a total of over thirty staff.

Leadership by Support

In building my team, particularly at 2IC Management, I decided that I had to help make them as good as possible with the talents they possessed. I believed that every person in our team could be a strong contributor if we focussed on what they were good at. Just as a football coach knows one particular player is good at going in and getting the ball and another is an outside receiver, you plan and strategise around what you have in your team.

I learned from some of my readings on business leadership and listening to Ric Payne about the concept of an inverted pyramid on leadership. If you asked most business owners their opinion on how the structure of a business should look, they would probably choose something very similar to the diagram below.

This is the traditional structure of leadership in business. Here the leaders are at the top of the pyramid. They are at the forefront leading by example, impressing clients, peers and other interested parties. In most situations, leaders

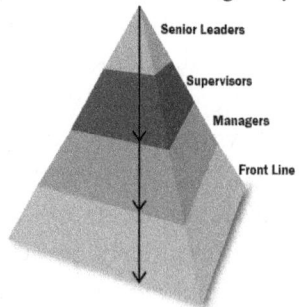

Senior Leaders

Supervisors

Managers

Front Line

act in this way because they believe this is how they should: they own the company so therefore they should be out the front promoting it. Quite often this is how businesses start, but to a large degree this model flourishes or is driven by the ego of the particular leader.

Although I was very comfortable leading from the front and promoting 2IC Management, I tended to concentrate on promoting us as a team and saw my role more as a pillar of support for everybody else in the business. The fact was, I had almost all of the combined experience in the team. I had filled just about every role that was required in the business at some stage, so who better to provide the support to everyone else. The leadership structure I promoted at 2IC Management looked more like this:

There were various ways, as you will read throughout this book, of how we promoted this concept of the 'inverted pyramid'. The result was that more front liners developed into managers, who in turn developed into supervisors and eventually made my role as the senior leader less critical. Living proof of this is the growth of Chris Stewart and Nick Vrees. Chris and Nick were former employees who started as juniors at 2IC Management and worked their way to be senior managers with full value add service capabilities and now are successful principals in their own practice. They were also kind enough to provide the testimonials at the beginning of this book.

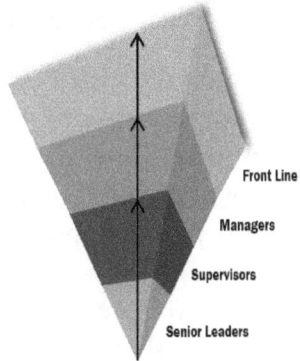

Write a Letter to Yourself and Share It

Writing a letter to yourself and sharing it with your team is an excellent strategy to focus your intentions and motivate your team to get engaged.

One way is to think about how you want your firm to look in five years' time:

- How many team members?
- How many clients?
- Where you are operating from?
- What the team looks like, who has advanced, who has retired etc.?
- What hours you are working?
- What amount of money you are earning?

Now write a letter to your spouse, partner, friend, parent or whoever is close to you, written in the future tense of five years' time. Crow about how well the firm has progressed, how well certain team members have grown, how good life is, and just as importantly about how much *fun* you are having.

Once you are happy with the vision of how your business looks, share it with the people close to you who you've identified, then share it with your team at a team meeting or make a special occasion out of it over a few drinks and ask them how they feel about the picture you've envisaged for the next five years. You will either get huge buy in from those around you, or you'll quickly work out who is not on board the bus with you.*

A lot of businesses talk about, and in fact work on implementing, Strategic Planning. However, unless you

---

* I have attached a copy of my own letter at Appendix L.

address the vision that you are aiming towards for your business, then the strategies you develop will themselves be misguided and without direction. Ric Payne often says, 'If you aim at nothing, you will hit it with a great deal of consistency.'

Some years ago, Ted became a client at Sims Richmond. Ted had invented a very valuable piece of machinery, a forerunner to cordless power tools. For many years, I'm told, his invention had superior performance to anything that could be purchased at the local hardware store. Ted's inventions resulted in an honorary degree in Engineering from University of Adelaide. This without having set foot in a classroom.

Unfortunately, Ted sought the advice of a solicitor on how to best launch his "super tool". The lawyer helped draw up documents to licence the rights to an international brand name in power tools, let's call them "PowerTools International".[†]

That was Ted's first big mistake, seeking direction from a lawyer and not a suitable accountant (we were not his accountant when this original deal was done). The second big mistake was not considering the vision for where his product would end up. He failed to see that his product would make obsolete the similar product already manufactured by PowerTools International.

The third and biggest mistake is that his lawyer didn't build into the contract a minimum sale or quantity a requirement for PowerTools International. As a consequence, a product that could have revolutionised the power tool industry worldwide sat on the shelf for the life of the licence agreement until technology caught up with his invention. Worse, Ted received no financial reward at all.

[†] Not their real company name.

I can recall countless, less critical decisions made by business owners with new and innovative ideas, investing vast amounts of time and small fortunes only to realise the idea won't work. The important point is to plan our strategies around our vision of the end result. As Stephen Covey, bestselling author of *The 7 Habits of Highly Effective People*,[‡] advises: begin with the end in mind.

Team Meetings

Many practitioners start out with an intention to hold regular meetings but are often the ones who book appointments over the scheduled times. I'm not talking about workflow meetings; these seem to have a medium level of success and are often managed by a senior at management level or thereabouts. I'm talking about chew the fat meetings discussing what is going well, what isn't and what can be done better for the team and then for the clients.

We had team meetings at 2IC Management scheduled every month and, although there were some days when they were cancelled, the overriding emphasis was to ensure that they were held. We appointed a different team member from the most junior to the most senior to chair the meeting. A suitably skilled touch typist would then take minutes. We would discuss:

- Team KPIs (see below).
- Agenda items raised by any team member.

[‡] Stephen Covey. *The 7 Habits of Highly Effective People.* Version 2.0 Singapore: Franklin Covey Co.

- Create implementation plans for strategies that may have been developed at Team Meetings or possibly Team Building Days (see below).
- Generally anything that made the place a better performer for clients or a better place to work.
- Almost always the next social event on our calendar, or why the alcohol supplies for Friday nights have been low or not cold!

Quite often I would just sit back and watch the interaction between the team and smile. It was quite infectious to hear our most junior employees contributing ideas that were accepted by all and then witness the enthusiasm that followed. Some team meetings were hard to close as there was so much chatter about what we were going to do and how we'd do it.[§]

Team KPIs

We developed a reporting spreadsheet that was circulated each month among all the team members, including principals. We had to complete data that reflected our performance and insights for the month just passed. Of particular importance were two KPIs that everybody was required to complete (measured from -5 to +5) being:

- How happy were you working at 2IC Management for the month? and,

---

[§] See later in this chapter, *Client WOW Ideas.*

- How happy do you think clients would be with what we did for the month?

This simple task gave huge insight into how a team member was travelling. As I mentioned earlier, every individual is different and needs to be treated as such. One team member may rate both questions as 1 month in, month out, whereas another may rate it 4.5 month in, month out, and they are both equally happy. It was when the 1 went to a zero or minus 1 or the 4.5 went to a 3 that it prompted me to have a chat and see what was bothering them. It was also a great opportunity for them to send me a message about a particular issue without them feeling like they were complaining or whinging. It worked a treat.

Furthermore, it's also good for team morale to holler when your average score across the team rises. This usually happens when we've had some significant wins that everyone in the team can then know about and feel part of.

Other KPIs we also listed were things like:

- Number of Wins achieved.
- Number of Failures.
- Impromptu Visits, Phone Calls, emails to clients (see later).
- Client Positive Feedback; and more importantly,
- Client Complaints (see later).

All these KPIs enabled us to discuss as a team what was working and what was going wrong and how we were going to manage it. I found that this process got my team not only on board, but it educated them about the business in general. This in turn made them feel much more valuable to the community and to themselves.

Patrick Lencioni, in his book *The Five Dysfunctions of a Team: A Leadership Fable*, talks about trust as being one of the key ingredients in a successful team. In particular, that team members can trust the ability to challenge each other without fear of retribution. In 2IC Management, the review of KPIs by all our team meant that juniors and seniors alike were able to air their views and review wins and losses without fear of reprisals. In essence, they were all equal and accountable to each other. Furthermore, for a junior team member or admin support to contribute an idea that is eventually adopted by the team does wonders for their self-esteem and builds the strength of the team. This has immeasurable benefits for team morale!⁵

As Sybil F. Stershic says in her book, *Taking Care of the People Who Matter Most: A Guide to Employee-Customer Care*, 'The way your employees feel is the way your customers will feel. And if your employees don't feel valued, neither will your customers.'

Team Building Days (TBDs)

We started team building days back in Sims Richmond when Dennis and I would arrange to take a team away for a weekend, usually somewhere local but far enough out of the city to feel a sense of having travelled. At these events, Dennis and I would present various topics, which would very rarely be of a technical nature. In those days we were

---

⁵ I have attached a copy of 2IC Management's Team KPI sheet at Appendix K.

stepping way outside the norm for accounting firm training sessions, even more so as they were being delivered by partners in their twenties. One particular topic I recall was about the difference between involvement and commitment. I asked our receptionist, who happened to be quite artistic, to recreate a cartoon I recalled from a training session I attended on Time Management. The cartoon showed a pig dressed as a chef with one wooden leg and a chicken also cooking fried eggs. Both had invested in a breakfast café business and the moral of the story was that the chicken was involved but the pig was *committed*. We didn't ask our team to be as committed as the pig, but it seemed to get the message across.

These trips away were fantastic for team bonding. We were also staying on site, so there were no problems with entertaining the troops and having to drive home intoxicated. On more than one occasion, the entertaining went well into the night and I can vividly remember lying in bed with a pillow over my head trying to drown out the dulcet sounds of our team belting out some tuneless song (and this was well before the days of Karaoke!). As Henry Ford is credited as saying, 'Coming together is a beginning; keeping together is progress; working together is success… If everyone is moving forward together, then success takes care of itself.'

At 2IC Management we developed some of our most powerful WOW Packs from these TBDs. I am a great fan of Dr Paddi Lund** and we identified his Critical Non-Essentials (CNEs) for our firm and went about creating systems to implement them.

We also had several moments where some team members (probably pushed forward by a few others) felt the time was

_____
** See Chapter 4, *Dr Paddi Lund*.

right to challenge the performance and lack of teamwork that had been put in by others. The TBDs were normally run on the basis that everybody had a right to present their thoughts on a particular issue at work or even a particular team member. But we always ensured that there was never any personal criticism of another. This was an important element to ensure everyone had the confidence to say what was on their mind and give input to the TBD. The effect was to create the right environment for issues to be raised and, just as importantly, an equally appropriate environment for it to be received. The TBDs certainly had a positive impact on our team and our business.

As Patrick Lencioni puts it in *The Five Dysfunctions of a Team: A Leadership Fable*, 'Trust is knowing that when a team member does push you they're doing it because they care about the team.'

Some of our best ideas also came from our support team, the ones who were not bogged down with compliance and technical issues. They were able to identify 'Great Customer Service' in other industries and we were able to take some of those strategies and implement them at 2IC Management. I've learned from following the likes of Sir Richard Branson, Founder of the Virgin Group of companies, and Herb Kelleher, CEO SouthWest Airlines, that you shouldn't compare your service or performance against your competitors, rather compare against the best performance and service offered by any business.

That ethos certainly helped us raise the bar.

Fun

Where do I start? If anything, I would have to admit that I was more than willing to sacrifice a full day's work for the team to have a bit of social time or knock off early for a drink. I'm sure I had some team members take advantage of this, but overall I would not change it because I know I received much more commitment and engagement from my team over the long-term.

Some of the fun activities we had included:

- Friday night drinks.
- End of Financial Year dinners with partners.
- Melbourne Cup afternoons. I mentioned this earlier at Sims Richmond and this tradition continued at 2IC Management. I even created a betting account at our local betting office* just for this day.
- Christmas breakup days. These generally started with breakfast followed by a bus trip, which included:
    —Lawn Bowls in the river town of Mannum.
    —Camel rides in the McLaren Vale wine district.
    —Archery in the Adelaide Hills.
    —Go-carts (with some F1-like spectacular crash scenes).
    —Great Race from Adelaide to Glenelg.

Sometimes the antics of these days gave the stirrers of our team (or me) ammunition to create a laugh at team meetings or while we were in smaller groups having a chat.

---

* The TAB.

These little quips helped keep a lighter atmosphere in the business, which I firmly believe is conducive to better performing employees and employers. It also gave a lighter atmosphere when dealing with clients as either I or our team members would chat about the fun we had at one of these events. I know the smiles and laughter that came from remembering these days was worth every cent lost in production hours and the actual cost of the event itself. It was paid back through people working harder and longer when needed, and the fact the team stayed working for me for longer periods of time. In seventeen years in business at 2IC Management, starting with one employee, I had six employees that between them totalled over sixty years of service for me.

Delegation

This is probably one of my pet issues. During my working life, I constantly lived it and constantly promoted it to clients. No single person will create a great business. That's a fact. You need a team. You need people, the right people.

I recently heard of a story where a mentor asked his students to look at the first two pages of Sir Richard Branson's autobiography, *Losing My Virginity*. He then asked his students to identify how many times Richard used the word 'I' and how many times the word 'we'. He used 'I' once and 'we' thirty times. Today, with world business leaders promoting teamwork, which by definition requires delegation, why are so many principals in practice, and for that matter business owners, so reluctant to delegate?

Our Staff Will Steal Our Clients:

Back in 1979, Dennis Sims and I decided how to counter the problem of staff leaving the firm and taking our clients with them, stealing them in fact. Thankfully, because of the serious nature of the issue we took it seriously, and it has never been a problem.[†] From almost the very beginning of Sims Richmond & Associates, we included in our employment contract an agreement that if a team member took a client within twelve months of leaving our firm they would pay one hundred cents in the dollar goodwill for the right. This meant that the annual fees paid the previous year by the client was the agreed value of their goodwill. We in fact turned something that was potentially very damaging to our business and made it a positive.

The client, by choosing to follow our team member to the new firm, was obviously happy with the service we had been providing at Sims Richmond & Associates. The clause in our employment contract also meant we could part company on a really good note, thanking the client and offering to help in any way with the transition.

We also found that the client felt comfortable coming back to us if they weren't happy with the service of the new firm. Furthermore, the departing team member arrived at the new firm (who inevitably paid the goodwill) with some kudos and we got paid a year's fees in advance.

[†] Except for one funny story: One employee left Sims Richmond to start up a new firm with several colleagues. We discovered he had poached a client and so confronted him, with the response: 'Our lawyer said the agreement wouldn't stand up in court.' The next day the ex-employee noticed Dennis in his reception taking down notes of all the firm's clients from their registered office board. When asked what he was doing, Dennis replied, 'Just jotting down the clients we are going to target.' We got the cheque the next day!

Some of these clients, who have gone with ex-employees, I still consider as close friends and even have regular social encounters with them.

They Won't Do as Good as Me!

Theodore Roosevelt said, 'The best executive is one who has the sense enough to pick good people to do what he wants done, and self-restraint enough to keep from meddling with them while they do it.'

The fear of executives and principals, however, is that team members won't do the job as good as them.

This fear could be right for a few reasons:

1. They probably won't do as good if you don't teach them.
2. If you don't empower them, they will not want to challenge themselves.
3. If you're that protective of your clients, your team will be constantly looking over their shoulder, which is a recipe for problems because everybody makes mistakes when working under constant pressure.

This fear will most likely be wrong for many reasons:

1. You're having a lend of yourself... you're not that good!
2. If you continue doing it all, you will either restrict yourself to a smaller number of clients to service or eventually let one or more down by taking shortcuts.
3. If they get ten jobs correct 80% of the time, this produces 800%; whereas you will not have time

to do eight jobs 100% correct. Once you learn as a business owner to accept that 80% correct is probably pretty good, you will in fact achieve a lot more.[‡] In Chapter 5, *Time Is Not Money… Value IS!* I explain how I originally placed too much emphasis on being 100% correct. This meant I dismissed employees who now, in hindsight, should have been retained because of their ability to build client relationships.

4. Unless you give them an opportunity, your team will eventually get disillusioned and leave. Then you will be stuck training the replacement to do the work of the departed.

It Will Take Me Longer to Show Them Than to Do It Myself

It most definitely will. It will take you longer to show them than to do it yourself the first time, and possibly the second, but after that you have freed up more time for yourself and now have a more valuable employee. This is your role, to delegate, and now that person can train the next person.

At Sims Richmond, a method we used to identify what tasks could be delegated was to have our various levels of team members keep a notepad on their desk (now probably an open electronic file) and every hour or so for a few days write down the tasks they have performed. At the end of the period they would review what they've written and highlight what tasks they have done that could be delegated. This way, by asking team members to list what they do, it becomes much easier to identify those specific tasks that don't require

---

[‡] Obviously, we don't want the 20% failure rate to be too critical, but the critical issues are actually what you review plus the implementation of systems to ensure quality assurance. The truth is you probably make close to the 20% errors yourself anyway.

their skill level, tasks that usually carry lower levels of risk for any potential mistakes that could be made. You will find, as will your clients, that it is easier to let go of certain tasks once you list them.

In my experience, most accounting offices have many tasks performed by the wrong people. Why would you have your senior accountants who can charge out at $200 plus per hour filing? Or worse, stuffing letters in an envelope?

The more your skilled people become skilled at delegating tasks, the more efficient your business becomes. Furthermore, the less-skilled team members grow their skills by being challenged by those above them. My first administration and reception employees at 2IC Management commenced work as keen people with great personalities but lacked confidence in performing tasks other than a bit of bookkeeping and providing a friendly smile when greeting someone. By delegating tasks to them, they grew in authority and later became genuine office managers.

Clients Always Want to See a Partner!

That's just rubbish. Clients only want to see a partner because they don't know any different and because that's how they have been told (probably by yourself) they would be treated.

Think about the instances when you have dealt with a lawyer or other professional. Would you rather only deal with a partner who charges the highest rate and won't be available until the next day because they are too busy serving other people, just like yourself. Or, would you prefer whoever can deal with your issue and solve your problem immediately at a much lower cost? If so, why wouldn't you recommend that to your clients?

At 2IC Management, we promoted the fact that our clients had a minimum of three people that were familiar with their accounting work and that there were one or two others in the firm that also understood their business and were available to assist with whatever they needed. Clients felt great when they walked through the office and five people greeted them with genuine recognition and interest. Far better for the client and your business than being greeted at the reception desk with, 'Sorry, who should I say is calling? Will he know what it's about?'

Clients actually don't mind at all when they get a call from a junior who says, 'Geoff and Chris were working on your file and they asked me to give you a call to chase up a missing bank statement.'

Another thing to keep in mind is that not only do you need to train your team, you also need to train your client. Here's an example of what I used to do. When I received a call from a client asking what their tax file number was, for instance, I would reply: 'I really don't know where to find some of this stuff on the system. Jennie is all over that, hold on while I transfer you through to her.' The next time they called they asked for Jennie.

Essentially, clients' work gets out the door quicker because your team are not held up waiting for the more senior person to call the client just to answer queries or to ask for missing information. This also helps counter the other very common complaint from clients: 'I just get used to one accountant and train him up and he leaves and now I have to train the new guy.' Many principals are very scared when a senior employee leaves. They are scared that either the client will follow the employee out of the door or that their departure might be the catalyst for the client to go elsewhere simply because they are fed up with constantly seeing new faces.

As a business owner, although it is paramount you try to make your firm a place where people want to stay forever, the fact of life is that they will leave one day. However, when the client has been dealing with a team of accountants and the partner is still the 'top guy', they are certainly more receptive when a senior person leaves the firm and the junior who has already had a relationship with them steps in. Once you have this structure in place with your clients, you have changed from being a commodity that's defined by one person into a firm that provides solutions, outcomes and results. The other benefit is you are no longer simply the accountant for a bunch of clients but a firm that becomes a much more saleable asset.

Leave You More Time to Do the Important Things

If you as the principal in the practice are tied up with the lower level work, then it's almost certain you will not have the time to devote to value add services or exploring other opportunities for either your clients or yourself.

I learned in the late 80s not to get involved in the compliance work of my business. As we were growing as a firm, I started delegating more and more and left my only involvement in compliance work to review work. One day I was informed by my key compliance manager that we were swamped with work and struggling to get it out in a suitable time. I promptly picked up one of the files she had and decided I would ease the load by completing that one. Two weeks later the file was still on my floor and not been started as I had constant urgent crises or value add services required by clients.

I learned a valuable lesson in priority management and I never picked up another compliance file after that.

Drive Every Employee to their Highest Level to Grow their Strengths and Improve Job Satisfaction

Team members that are comfortable with a certain level will settle and those that can rise to the occasion can keep growing and do higher level work for you.

It also enables the support team to do work often left to qualified accountants that frees them to do higher level work. This also gives support team members so inclined a more purposeful role that they will enjoy and help them develop as productive members of your team.

Everybody likes to have pride in doing a good job. That pride rises as they perform well on more challenging and valuable work. That's got to be good for team morale. Therefore, don't steal the limelight or praise for a great result for a client. Instead, put the team member on a pedestal and praise them for doing well. As Larry Bossidy, CEO of Allied Signal, said, 'I am convinced that nothing we do is more important than hiring and developing people. At the end of the day you bet on people, not on strategies.'

I always looked for opportunities to give praise to my team member in front of clients. If the client was happy with the service my team had provided, comments like, 'Don't thank me, thank Jordan,' helped to build a stronger relationship with both the client and the employee.

I've also gone into a number of client meetings intent on praising my team for the great work they'd done for the client, saying things like, 'I have had Jordan looking at the issues we are trying to solve for you and he has come up with a great way of getting what we need based on this particular strategy.' The fact was, I had sent Jordan off to research what I had strategised but I didn't need the personal praise, the firm did. The response was often, 'That's great! Thank you and thanks Jordan.'

Win-win!

'It's the End of the World as We Know It!'

We actually ran a seminar for clients in our offices with this as the title, It's the End of the World as We Know It! We were trying to explain the benefits of systems and delegation and had a real-life example to illustrate.

Unfortunately for me I was the real-life example. At one of our TBDs I strained my back doing the set-up carting audio-visual equipment and supplies before the gang arrived. The upshot was I spent six weeks in hospital after a serious mishap where an infection was introduced into my spinal cord. I could hardly walk for three months and did not attend our offices at all. I was only able to start attending over the following three months, and even then only on a part-time basis.

Thankfully, we did not lose one client directly because of my hospitalisation and incapacity.§ The main reason we didn't lose clients was because none of them were inconvenienced. Their work was being handled by my team and if for some reason it wasn't up to date they had an understanding of the situation and were not caused any harm or distress.

§ We did lose one client during this time, but he was well on the way out before I was incapacitated.

At the seminar, my team delivered a summary of all the systems we had established and the delegation that had made our practice seemingly bulletproof during my absence. As it turned out, my accident wasn't the end of the world!

This incident was also a further lesson on delegation because I had a number of team members step out of their comfort zone and present to the clients that evening. They told how they had helped create the systems and how they were able to continue delivering value add services to our clients even in my absence.

Not only did this help the team grow in confidence, but it was another opportunity to showcase them to clients and further emphasize that 2IC Management was a team that was there to help clients rather than them relying on any one individual.

Another interesting phenomenon was highlighted during this experience for me. I often told clients that part of the benefits we brought as business consultants was that because we have worked so close to so many different businesses, we saw what worked for some and what didn't for others. Oftentimes I found myself almost on autopilot having been through similar circumstances before.

Such an instance happened while I was in hospital. I had the unusual circumstance where two of my clients were involved in a sale of a business from one to the other. I had been involved in the preliminaries with both clients prior to my back injury, but the final touches on their agreement needed finalising while I was hospitalised.

The vendor, Carol, arranged to visit me in hospital and I gave her some important advice and direction from my hospital bed. Now, on the surface this doesn't seem too special, and Carol was not concerned at the time. After all, it was my back that was hurt, not my head or brain. However, I was in considerable pain at the time and I was under a fairly heavy dosage of morphine. This meant at times I had little recollection of what was happening from day-to-day.

After I was back on my feet (literally), I spoke to Carol about the sale of her business. I became aware that I had given her advice on certain aspects of the business deal that I couldn't remember because of the morphine. I actually had to ask her what advice I had given. I was very relieved to hear that what I had suggested was exactly what I would have suggested at that time while free from painkillers.

I confessed that I did not recall the specific conversation, but did confirm that I was happy with what I had advised while on 'autopilot'.

Empowerment

There is a big difference between empowerment and delegation. If you truly empower your team they will explode with ideas and efforts to impress you and your clients. Empowerment encourages your team to perform to their best without the pressure of failure.

As Simon Sinek, motivational speaker and author of *Start With Why: How Great Leaders Inspire Everyone to Take Action*, said, 'When people are financially invested, they want a return. When people are emotionally invested, they want to contribute.'

One story I have relayed many times was when I was at a footy team meeting. Our coach had arranged for the iconic

Mike 'Swamp Fox' Patterson to give us a pep talk before an important game. Mike told two stories on that occasion.

The first was about the jar of fleas. He explained that once you put fleas in a jar they will jump and ping the lid of the jar for some time. Eventually they will stop hitting the lid because they can't reach any higher. Once they stop hitting the lid, you are able to remove the lid rest assured that the fleas won't jump out because they have set their own limit of what they can achieve.

Mick's message was that, unfortunately, too many people either set their own limits or have them set by others and never achieve their full capabilities. As business owners we are, amongst many things, charged with the responsibility of pushing those we employ to create new highs. Do this and you will build more successful employees and also reap the rewards of their efforts.

The second story was a about the USA Olympic Sprint Team. At a training session, the Sprint Team were doing one hundred metre sprints and jogging back to the start line. The team were instructed to now give it their best. 'We want your fastest time,' the coaches said, and recorded their times. Then they jogged back to the start and were instructed to give only 90% this time. What happened was astonishing. As a whole, the recorded times for only 90% effort were better than when they were asked to give it their all.

It seemed that the times for the whole team were best when they took the pressure off and were not expected to be best. The message therefore is this: Empowering your team is giving them the freedom to outperform but not expecting miracles or even their best effort. Just watch, and they will produce better than you expect and most probably the best.

Another philosophy I learned along the way was to

distinguish between the mistake and the person. As Coleman Hawkins, jazz musician, said, 'If you don't make mistakes, you aren't really trying.'

Therefore, by acknowledging a mistake as an outcome as opposed to a personal failure, I was able take the pressure off my team, just like the two examples above. When team members are not afraid to make mistakes, when they don't feel the pressure of perfectionism, they don't get into the habit of constantly doubting themselves or looking over their shoulder.

Instead, they get into the great habit of simply trying to get the best results they can.

Fun Breaks!

Just like the USA Olympic Sprint Team, no-one can work at 100% effort all the time.

My team were quite often working whatever times were required to get the job done. Lunch breaks often turned into the time it took to inhale a sandwich and five o'clock usually meant it was time for another coffee. By encouraging the team to take a fun break, they didn't need to be concerned that the boss might walk pass and hear them chatting about the footy or their social calendars.

I remember one day in my office with a client when the open plan area exploded with laughter. The client paused and waited in anticipation for my response. He was quite taken back when I said, 'You know that is one of the best sounds I hear in this office. If they're happy, I know they are enjoying working here.' I knew I had a good team and that they were good at their jobs. The fact that they were happy at the same time was another win-win.

This attitude also works in reverse. When employees consider leaving their job, they probably get to thinking that the grass may be greener at an alternative firm. However, if they knew their current employer was happy to support fun breaks and they knew that was because they were committed to producing results at other times, they'd most likely doubt that this type of treatment would be available elsewhere.

Fun breaks mean the grass is greener on our side of the fence.

Knowledge Workers

One of the key principles of value pricing is that you and your team are not process workers but 'Knowledge Workers'. If you anoint your team with this philosophy, they will respond with outstanding performances.

The difference between a bookkeeper and an accountant should be this: the accountant uses the knowledge first gained from his/her education plus what they have learned in creating value for clients and solving their problems. If they do not bring these attributes, then their rates should be charged at bookkeepers' rates. Again, reinforcing this to your team will increase their pride in what they do, which will mean increasing the fee you charge for their services.

Eventually your team, as mine, will insist on the fee that needs to be charged because they are confident in the value they are bringing and are proud of what they have created.

Recently I had the experience of helping a home renovation business with their marketing strategies and we noticed the effective reverse of this strategy. The renovation team were aware of the time effort and resources they put into the result they created for their clients, which justified in their minds the price they charged. We then worked with this team to turn their focus on the value or benefits they provided to their clients to great effect. Previously, the sales team felt justified in the price of their service but were uncomfortable that it was expensive. By focussing on benefits and value they provided, the team could then feel comfortable that their clients were getting a return on their investment.

After sitting down with their team and discussing the extra mile this business went for their clients, both the team and we as their consultants were able to realise the value they actually provided that their competitors didn't. One example was their willingness to guarantee that, after completion of the initial demolition work, the remainder of the client's home would be as clean as or cleaner than when they first arrived. As a home owner undertaking a renovation, one of the big issues is the dust and mess that tradies leave behind. This was a value proposition that the team had taken for granted but one their clients would attribute great value to.

For any business to have pride in what they produce, the team need to believe in it. By identifying the value our home renovation client gave to their clients we were able to help the team feel comfortable with the sale. Equally, by treating your team as Knowledge Workers, they will have pride in what they do and what your firm produces for clients. They will walk tall when delivering this to clients.

Think Time and Team Brainstorming

With our attitude of not letting a set of financials leave the office without a comment our accountants needed to stop and think. Rather than having a pressure cooker approach to finish the tax return and get it out the door your team will discover opportunities to do something extra for your client… Make An Impact: More Time, More Money, More Fun. The end result is you helped the client and made you and the firm look good. Again, happy clients mean more referrals, more growth and a greater value of your practice.

I estimate that team brainstorming produced in excess of $200,000 in fees for my practice over an eighteen-month period, simply because a few of my team started chatting about what we could do for our clients. Furthermore, because of our team brainstorming strategy, our clients were better off by literally millions of dollars.

One such strategy revolved around self-managed super-funds, which at the time were only implemented by larger accounting firms on a case by case basis when someone in their team happened to think about it. I have encountered countless new clients that unfortunately missed this tax-saving strategy because nobody discussed it with them. When we realised the value we could bring to our clients, we literally went through our whole client base and identified those who could benefit. This is just one example of the benefits of team brainstorming.

Other results, though not as impressive but by no means insignificant, were achieved quite regularly on individual cases where team brainstorming identified solutions to a client's problem. I would often walk into an open plan office of several accountants to find them pens down and facing each other brainstorming a solution.

When showing clients or new team members around the office, I would always refer to this area as the 'brains trust'.

The benefit of Think Time and Team Brainstorming to team engagement is the feeling that they are contributing value for the client. There is a much greater sense of purpose in helping a client achieve More Time, More Money and More Fun. Plus, it makes your job so much more enjoyable than simply preparing a tax return. The first helps create history whereas the second simply records it.

Developing Systems

Every accounting practice needs to have systems to operate efficiently. However, if it is left to the partners or principals, then the systems will tend to be structured around leadership vision and big picture processes. In my role as an advisor to other accounting firms, I am often amazed at how little systems are used in middle tiered firms, other than the systems designed by auditors that tend to revolve around issues dictated from their head office and more often than not hinder the overall performance of the business rather than supplementing and improving it.

When I moved 2IC Management out from under the wing of Sims Richmond to our own offices, I urgently needed to employ a receptionist and office administrator. The biggest problem was not finding staff, but that we weren't yet a big enough organisation to keep them both busy. But we knew we would grow to be big enough, and eventually we did.

So what I did in the meantime was to empower my two new recruits to develop systems for everything they could think of for the office. This was the foundation for our 'End of the World' seminar mentioned earlier. Because my two new team members, Jennie and Amanda, had no pre-conceived idea what was important and what wasn't in an accounting practice, they went about creating systems and operations manuals with a clean slate. If they saw a problem in the office, they created a system.[*]

They were also empowered to come up with client Wow Packs or, even more simply, to think about how we could make a positive impression. Over the years at 2IC Management, I constantly encouraged our team to create new ideas to wow our clients. The culture grew such that the team would be constantly on the look for new ideas. We developed WOWs from discussions at team meetings, TBDs, or even over coffee during the week or a wine at Friday night drinks. Below are some of examples of what the team came up with.

Client WOW Ideas

Client WOW ideas uphold the philosophy of Kevin Stirtz, author of *More Loyal Customers*,[**] that, 'Every contact we

---

[*] See Chapter 9, *Systems*
[**] Kevin Stirtz, *More Loyal Customers: 21 Real World Lessons to Keep*

have with a customer influences whether or not they'll come back. We have to be great every time or we'll lose them.'

With this in mind, our team developed some great ideas for keeping up the WOW factor and our customers happy. Though not rocket science, they are very effective tools to encourage your customers to come back.

Menu in Reception

Over the years at 2IC Management, we did a lot of R&D (Rip off & Duplicate) when we saw a good idea. Although a bit of copying was involved, the important part from our end was to make it our own as something to implement into our daily business.

One of the first things we did was to incorporate menus into our reception. I think we heard about the idea from a RAS or Principa member, but we created our own menu at one of our TBDs. Each menu was printed every morning with the name of the visitor at the head. It didn't matter whether it was a client, a prospect, another accountant, a banker, or even someone from the ATO, everyone got one. On the menu we had a variety of teas and coffees, from short black to lattes, various biscuit selections, baguettes, soft drinks, and alcoholic beverages.

But it didn't stop at food and drink items. We also offered other assistance such as:

- Phone chargers for visitors while they were in the meeting.
- Umbrellas to walk to their car if it was raining.
- Answer their phone calls while in the meeting

Your Customers Coming Back, Stirtz Group LLC, 2008.

Furthermore, the menu had our performance standards printed on the back[††], things such as:

- How quickly we promised to return calls.
- What the client could expect when they visited us.
- How we would deal with their work.
- Details of how we serviced them as a team and not simply one contact person.

Doughnut Packs

Another idea that was developed at our TBDs was doughnut packs. Again, I think we R&D'd this idea from someone else and put our 2IC Management stamp on it. Wording along the lines of 'You look after the business and we will look after the Dough!' was printed on packaging that we filled with doughnuts and gave to clients on special occasions and Client Team Visits (another WOW idea).

Initially we had some keen team members bake some special cakes, but eventually we decided on buying doughnuts from a nearby bakery.

Give Your Client $10,000!

No, we didn't actually give our client $10,000, but we certainly gave a lot of clients the chance to win $10,000.

At one of our TBDs, we discussed the highs and lows of our clients' relationship with us. Our aim was to make as many highs as possible. Of particular note was the low point when our client received a tax payable assessment from the ATO. Although this wasn't any fault of our making, it did

---

[††] Our menu and performance standards are included at Appendix M.

affect our relationship with our client. We asked ourselves: How can we make this less of a down moment for the client?

Our solution was to include with the ATO assessment a Lotteries Scratchy Ticket that gave the client a chance to win up to $10,000. So, with every letter we sent out to our clients with a tax payable assessment, we spent an extra dollar and included the scratchy ticket with the following paragraph:

> *We have enclosed a small gift with our compliments. With a bit of luck, it might help soften the pain, clear your tax debt or, even better, leave some extra for you! Please let us know if you have a win.*

We discussed the potentially huge PR result and marketing opportunity would be if a client actually won big. Our biggest disappointment was that we didn't have any client win anything too big to get excited about. Or so we think. Perhaps someone had a big win but was worried we would want a share of it!

Client Team Visits

Continuing the team approach to serving clients, we approached clients to assess whether they'd be open to some of our team visiting their offices, factory or place of business. The reception by clients was fantastic. They discovered that not just the principal of our firm was interested in what they did, but three or four other people wanted to know more about them and their business.

We arrived usually with about four team members and

a box of our branded doughnuts and pre-arranged coffee orders. More often than not, the clients were proud to show our team around their premises, introducing us to their employees, explaining their processes being carried out, and often bragging about their successes.

Another emphasis on the team approach was that I wasn't always present at these visits. I found that a great way to build engagement with clients was the engagement between the client and the firm, not necessarily the client and principal.

Recognition

Team Reviews

Team reviews were one of the hardest items I found to schedule throughout the year. Missing them had a huge negative effect on morale and running them, although quite stressful and overwhelming, was a very important ingredient in building my team.

At 2IC Management, we ran six monthly reviews. The first was a performance review that did not consider remuneration, unless it was requested by the team member. The second performance review discussed remuneration.

On both occasions, we attempted to get the 'elephant in the room' out in the open. We asked our team members to complete a questionnaire where they assessed themselves. The more confident and honest members would fess up about their shortcomings during the period, which made it easy to discuss with them the way forward. It was also easier to remind someone of something they may have forgotten rather than to confront them with a poor performance slap. I found this subtle approach helped to nurture a more mature and less threatening discussion.

More important, however, was giving recognition to achievements, growth and development and help set goals for the future. These goals then set a format for the next review.

Team Awards

Our KPI sheets gave individuals the right to shout out loud their wins. So we made a point of discussing them in front of everyone. I stressed that if we had a win with a client we would highlight the contribution of any team member who provided input. The result was that energy grew within the team and team members started building on the achievements of others.

We also had monthly awards for best performer who received the office star trophy and got to display it proudly on their desk for the month. It didn't matter how often someone won this award, they always showed pride for being recognised. Let's face it, we all like to get a pat on the back from our peers.

We also had a bit of fun by awarding the 'Turkey Award', which also came with a suitable trophy. And yes, the Boss was also eligible and I had the Turkey Award in pride of place on my desk on quite a few occasions. This award was never about making mistakes, but more about doing something silly that others could laugh about.

OK, I'll fess up on one of my Turkey Awards. I had booked a flight for a new employee to attend a client visit interstate with me. I had actually arranged this before the employee started with us, having discussed it during our interview process. For reasons still unknown to all, including me, this particular employee resigned within three days of commencing work at our firm. This meant that I had a ticket with an airline that I could not get a refund on or change the name of the passenger. Always thinking of a solution, I decided to fly under 'John Smith's' name to Brisbane at a later date for a conference. The flight from Adelaide went without any problems. I arrived quite early at Brisbane Airport for the return flight home, but as I wasn't booked under my name I wasn't able to visit the Qantas Club. So I decided to get out my laptop and do a bit of work in the café adjacent the departure gates.

I was under the impression that my flight home was the last for the day, but when I looked at the departure time I discovered my boarding call was some five minutes earlier. I raced to the gate to be told that the plane had departed. I was also asked, 'Where were you, Mr Smith? We called your name quite a few times.'

I couldn't really admit that I didn't notice the call because that wasn't my name. I was also quite nervous as to how I was going to get another flight without ID. Well, karma was certainly with me as the flight attendant found me another flight, which actually got me home faster than the one I missed. Somehow, I think I really should have been a candidate for the Star Award that month.

In Front of Clients

If I was ever going to convince clients that they were in safe hands with a team approach rather than 'just dealing with the partner', I needed to build their confidence in my team.

I therefore always looked for opportunities to show off my team whenever I could. If I attended a client meeting with a team member and they had done all the number crunching for the presentation, I insisted that the team member do the presentation. I would make comments to strengthen the proposal we were presenting, but would also ask the team member questions so they could answer them in front of the client and build their authority with the client.

This tactic alone has seen many of my team grow in confidence. They would not have had the confidence to deliver to the client in the first instance without my presence, but because of our many repeat meetings I would almost see myself as a spectator, confident that they could take on new client assignments without my physical presence.‡‡ My role then became the mentor or coach. The flow-on benefit was more hours for me!

Your Employees are Your Most Valuable Asset

During my two years of hell at a mid-tier firm, previously mentioned, I actually did work with a few really promising accountants. One accountant in particular was quite early in her career. She was always keen to help, never shelved jobs that were outside her comfort zone, always had an attempt and sought assistance to get the job done. I found her attitude a lot different to many young accountants who hid the job file in their bottom drawer and hoped no-one came looking for it. I'm sure many accountants have had occasions where the client calls to see how a certain project is going and when you eventually track down who you asked to look after it you find they have done nothing.

---

‡‡ Several of my key employees, such as Chris Stewart, went from being my support in client meetings to being their trusted advisor. So much so that when Chris left he had a significant fee base that wanted to follow him, and for which he gladly paid me goodwill for their patronage (see Chris' testimonial at the front of this book).

One day one of my loyal clients, Mark, told me that Carol was the best accountant he had dealt with. I know he was saying this 'with the exception of me', but he was clearly impressed with her willingness and 'here to serve' approach. The upshot was that my loyal client had never been impressed with the mid-tier firm and eventually left. What I discovered later, although I knew the client was leaving to join my former employee Chris, was that he had discovered through some coincidental circumstances Carol was also leaving to work for Chris. I often wonder if this was the catalyst to push him to make the final decision.

Tear Up Your Time Sheets Event

Always the pioneer, 2IC Management was one of the first firms to tear up its time sheets. I was acknowledged by VeraSage Institute in the USA for our decision and the presentation to our clients was posted on their website. BRW also interviewed me regarding our trailblazing strategy (I'll discuss more about time sheets in Chapter 4, *Time Sheets*). Rather than just change the way we billed our clients, we chose to announce it with a presentation. We hired a seminar room at the picturesque Adelaide Oval and had a ceremonial tearing up of time sheets in front of our clients.

At this presentation, I gave a speech and had a Power-Point presentation where I told my clients upfront that: 'For years I had the opinion that our clients were the most important ingredient in our business, but I am sorry to tell you today that this is not the case. I have decided the most important ingredient is my team, because without them we cannot serve you and eventually you will disappear from lack of service.'

I then went on to introduce each team member and give

each one of them a rap. As Ian Hutchinson, author of *People Glue*, said, 'Your number one customers are your people. Look after employees first and then customers last.'

Best Sale Opportunity for Your Goodwill

As previously explained, by anointing your team as the best way to handle your clients' needs, you build a strong relationship between your client and your key team members. It also builds a stronger relationship between you and your team because each member enjoys the relationship and looks to you for support. The end result is that you ultimately have a ready-made market to sell your goodwill.

The team member is happy, the client is happy and you will have cleared some debt or saved some funds for retirement.

Financial Recognition

Job Satisfaction

Team engagement is much more important than remuneration. Results on surveys[§§] of job satisfaction from all industries indicate the following, with the order of priority for job satisfaction being lowest at 1) and highest at 10):

1. Respectful treatment of all employees at all levels.
2. Trust between employees and senior management.

[§§] *The Society for Human Resource Management (SHRM) 2015 Survey.*

3. Benefits overall.
4. Compensation/pay overall.
5. Job security.
6. Relationship with immediate supervisor.
7. Opportunities to use skills and abilities in your work.
8. Immediate supervisor's respect for employee ideas.
9. Organisation's financial stability.
10. Performance is recognised by management.

As can be seen, money and remunerations rates some way down the list.

I learned some time ago that remuneration for staff should be set not necessarily at the best in the competition, but such that it is never at a level that is an issue for your employee. This I would consider 'Appropriate Remuneration'. Once an employee is paid appropriate remuneration, you need to deal with all the other priorities for job satisfaction and engagement.

Incentives and Rewards

I'm probably a bit out of line with a lot of people in this area, but my logic is supported by the list above and my observation of behavioural outcomes.

I'll now discuss some examples to help support my opinion.

Printing Company Client:

Many years ago, I had a request from a client regarding setting up an incentive scheme. The lessons of this are so important I have often used this example in consulting to clients, coaching clients and mentoring my team.

The client asked me to help design an incentive scheme. I asked what he wanted to achieve out of the scheme. His response was to get more production from his team. I then asked two further questions:

1. What productivity are you getting now? and,
2. What productivity do you want?

I can still remember the confused look on the client's face. He had trouble answering both questions. I also asked him a third question, whether he had ever had a discussion with his team about what he expected their production to be?

I guess when he couldn't answer what productivity he wanted, he was unlikely to have had a discussion with his team about it. So, we set up a means of measuring what production he was getting and then asked him to talk to his team. By simply telling his team how many hours of productivity he expected, the results were simply amazing!

The client measured the productivity performance and monitored it monthly. Just talking to his team about the results accelerated his productivity and bottom line profit by 200% and he didn't spend a cent on any incentives.

The underlying lesson is that you cannot expect your team to perform to your expectations if you do not set clear guidelines on what you want.

The other factor that comes in here is the 'Hawthorne Effect'.[**] I have witnessed for years the improved results of clients who monitor their KPIs and results, and often proffered the benefits before I was informed of this recognised phenomenon. It is a proven fact that by monitoring results on a regular basis you will improve those results.

[**] See Chapter 10, *Monitoring—The Hawthorne Effect.*

Sims Richmond Incentives—The Potential Negative
Effect of Incentives!:

At Sims Richmond, we devised some incentives whereby
team members would receive a bonus if they achieved certain targets.

The scheme was abolished sometime later when we found
it promoted individual performances rather than team ones.
Even though we had an overriding criterion that team results had to be met before individual incentives were paid,
we discovered that some more senior team members were
hoarding work and doing it all themselves rather than delegating to more junior team members. The result was that
we had some employees looking for work while others were
working late to get through their work. This was not a good
ingredient for team morale and productivity.

Team Incentives:

If you are going to provide incentives, I recommend that
they are team oriented. This benefit is to bind the team together to achieve the results you outline.

Whether the reward is money, or some other form of
thank you like a voucher for dinner or a bottle of champagne,
will depend on a number of factors, but the main foundation
is whether your team members are receiving appropriate
remuneration.

Ad Hoc Rewards and Celebrations for Success:

Once you have your team on appropriate remuneration,
you can get some great buy-in and team building by celebrating wins as a team. Highlight the win, who contributed,
what it means to the client and the firm, and then crack

the champagne, set the agenda for a luncheon, dinner or whatever suits.

For individuals, I recommend ad hoc rewards. A pat on the back or recognition is one of the highly sought after ingredients of a good job. Equally a bonus that comes out of left field is usually more appreciated than someone receiving a bonus that they 'expect'.

I have also witnessed several incentive schemes appropriately designed and relevant to both employees and the business when first implemented. But over time things change, such as the size of the business, margins required to cover base remuneration packages, and the general economy as a whole. The problem the business owner faces then is how to take back or adjust an incentive package that a particular employee has become accustomed to and may be planning a Christmas holiday based on that incentive.

For instance, one particular client purchased a business where their sales team were paid commissions on a set formula. However, the economy dramatically changed and the business went backwards. Yet because of the commission-based formula they stuck to, one salesperson was earning super income when the company was actually experiencing large losses.

Mistakes Happen

Mistakes are a process, not a person. Therefore reward the person, improve the process.

One of the big things in dealing with your team is to ensure that you give both positive and negative feedback on a regular basis. Both are equally important, but how to give negative feedback is very important. If your team are singled out for mistakes they will develop a fear of failure and be reluctant to stretch their boundaries (as discussed in the sub-chapter *Empowerment*).

Therefore, I developed the habit of always referring to mistakes as the process rather than the person. Rather than, 'You did this wrong!' I preferred to talk in such a manner as, 'These sums don't add up!' or We can't give this to the client like this!'.

It also helped to emphasise how are *we* going to ensure *we* do not make this mistake for a client again?

Understand Your Team

I mentioned earlier the team KPI reports that indicated how the team was travelling. On top of this, I found it beneficial to talk to the people who had their ear to the ground. Every firm has somebody like this, and usually they are the ones that care a lot about what is happening within team, so much so they are often torn between the loyalty to the team and to the firm. I found that raising topics with these team members allowed them to open up without betraying confidences of other team members.

I had one such team member, Trish, who was always there to act as the go-between. She helped me solve many team issues, although sometimes there were issues that were much harder to deal with.

A classic example of not knowing where the team was at was again during my employment at a mid-tier firm.

This firm created a Survey Monkey questionnaire to measure team engagement. Each year the firm would rate right up there compared to the rest of Australia and the partners would get on their soapbox and brag to their team at how great their team engagement was. I was quite amazed, as I heard the comments and innuendos from the team and saw the massive exodus of employees.

When I asked team members what they thought of the Survey Monkey results, they simply laughed. 'If I answered any questions the way I wanted to, the survey would then ask another question. I was worried this would identify me so I changed my original answer.'

Computers are nowhere near capable of replacing human interaction when it comes to emotional intelligence. The real issue wasn't that the survey didn't give accurate results, but that it actually drove a bigger wedge between their staff and the partners. Every meeting an employee had with a partner was therefore prefaced by the partner thinking the employee was 'engaged' and the employee continuing to say what they thought the partner wanted to hear… until they decided to leave.

Hierarchy

Open Door Policy

How many businesses have an 'Open Door Policy' but only ever give it lip service?

I can plead guilty to this in the earlier days at Sims Richmond when I was flat out doing it and working *in* the business rather than *on* it.*** I discovered that it's not that the principal doesn't want to discuss the issues a team member may have, it's just that they are too busy to stop and think about how important it is. As we have pointed out, a key issue for staff and clients is their perception of being important to you. I know of several occasions that staff have left their employ because the boss 'Didn't give a shit about them.' I was lucky enough on one occasion to be able to convince an employee to change their mind when they handed in their resignation. It all revolved around their perception of the value we considered they brought to the firm.

So, whatever you do, if a team member asks for a chat, *always* take the time to meet them. If you feel it is a crucial point, go for a coffee, beer or lunch away from the office so the meeting is on equal terms.

If the team member asks to have a chat about issues and it is in your office, you will always have a dominating position at the meeting. If I ever got the idea a team member had some real issues that needed my support in I would always prefer to say, 'Shall we get a bite to eat to discuss this?' or, 'Would you like to grab a coffee across the road?'

If it wasn't that important to them, the employee would simply say they were happy to just come in for a few minutes. But if it was critical, they always preferred to meet away from the office. Sometimes we even made it a secret meeting so other team members were not aware that they had any personal problems.

Fair and Square

No valuable employee really respects a boss who they can

***

*** To use a phrase from Michael Gerber's book, *The E-Myth: Why Small Businesses Don't Work and What to Do About It.*

wrap around their fingers. They are just immature and prefer to play games than work. They will eventually think they are better off at another firm and will leave you for no reason other than greed.

I mentioned that at salary review time we asked our team to submit a written report and to include their expected salary. Usually their expectations were similar to mine. If they were slightly higher, I would usually point this out but often agree to increase it to their expectations. The really good employees that asked for less than I expected were given praise and an amount greater than they expected.

There was one occasion when I had a very important member of my team set a salary expectation way in excess of her then current salary. Her request was in a different stratosphere compared to my expectations and caused me a lot of angst for some time before we had our review meeting.

I was troubled for days and even sought feedback from a number of different sources to ensure I wasn't way out of line. This employee at this stage of her career was probably a bit naïve with regard to salaries (she did grow to be one of my most valued and loyal team members, however, and her salary eventually reflected that). The last thing I wanted to do was upset her, or for her to think she was hard done by, and cause her to hand in her resignation.

I approached the meeting with a great deal of uncertainty. Did she really think she was that much underpaid at present? I needed to be honest and maintain my integrity, so once the meeting had taken place I explained that I was quite taken aback with her expectations and asked how she arrived at such a figure. As it turns out she had done some homework and simply asked the wrong people or researched the wrong areas. She was probably more embarrassed than me, and in the end we had a good laugh. We reached agreement and she stayed with the firm until she had her first child.

Does Tough Work?

Just as a footy coach needs to treat different players with different degrees of toughness, being tough can work with some team members.

I remember being approached by a player when I was coaching football telling me, 'Richo, you're a great coach but you're not tough enough on us. You need to lose your cool and get stuck into us more!'

I also remember one of my former partners giving me very similar advice, something along the lines: 'No matter how you treat them, they will eventually shaft you.'

That partner built a lot of respect from our employees but not necessarily as an employer, rather for his skills as an accountant. I also question whether we ever really built a team under this model.

Needless to say, his firm hand built some strong loyalty from key employees in future business ventures he created, so perhaps they were the type of players that needed a rev up from the coach every now and again. I later got to know several key employees he took from one business to another who would openly say how tough he was, how aggressive he was, and how tight he was, usually followed by a chuckle.

However, even with these comments he obviously built some great loyalty because they were willing to follow him from one business to another. I guess tough love does work with some people.

Benefits of a Flat Team Structure

Obviously, there is a need for structure in your organisation with more experienced people controlling the work that needs that experience. However, what I see too often is good juniors being stifled in growth because they do not get a shot at the more challenging work.

Too often partners will protect higher end work because they want to maintain ownership and control of their client. Alternatively, managers fail to delegate their work because they believe it will dilute their importance on the job.

I was told by a partner of a Big 4 firm of an actual example of this. This partner specialised in a tax related topic and was renowned through accounting circles in South Australia, having presented papers at tax conferences on the topic. One of his Adelaide partners was concerned about losing control of a particular client, so he instructed a partner from Sydney to visit Adelaide to consult to the client. That may seem fine from the outside, but it cost the client an extra $100 plus per hour for the exercise![†††]

In my experience, the benefits of having a structure where all team members are involved at various levels of client work are better client service, tighter team unity, and continual education of all team members.

[†††] I will expand my views on this later in the book.

~4~

Client Engagement

*'The most important single ingredient in the
formula of success is knowing how to get along
with people.'*

Theodore Roosevelt

Is a Loyal Client Enough?

There is a major difference between having a loyal client and a client that is engaged. Clients that are engaged are much more likely to refer others and will take up offers when you send them out.

What would you prefer? A client that stays with you for twenty years at an average fee of $5,000 per annum, or one that sings your praises whenever possible and refers you $5,000 worth of new clients each year. Obviously the latter!

I had one client that started with me early at Sims Richmond. Carol only required me to prepare a personal tax return and her fee would have been approximately $100 per annum. She came to me as a referral from her brother, Doug, who was one of my longest-term clients and who was very happy to sing my praises when he had the opportunity. Now, Carol knew a lot of people and mixed in a circle that was the 'to be seen set' in Adelaide. She referred Margie, who was probably one of my most enjoyable clients to deal with over the years. Margie referred Carol, Bob, Carol and Carol, (all separate businesses), eventually married and we then looked after her husband, Michael. All in all, this group of clients combined annual fees would have been well in excess of $100,000 per annum with other large one-off assignments along the way. Were they engaged? Hell yeah!

We therefore recognised the need for client engagement and set about introducing systems and strategies to achieve this.

One story makes me proud and is an example of the engagement we had with our clients. One client was putting the final touches on an extension to his hotel when another of my clients dropped in to say hello. The two clients knew each other and started a chat about the renovations. The hotelier made a comment to the other client that he was trying to come up with a suitable name for a new room he had added as part of the extension. The other client also knew how much we had helped the hotelier and made a suggestion: 'You've mentioned before how much help Geoff has been to you over the years, why don't you call it the 'Richmond Room'

The hotelier responded, 'Brilliant!' and for a number of years I had a room in a hotel named after me.

I can tell you that whenever I went to the hotel I always entered through the door with leadlight window emblazoned with "Richmond Room". I was very proud to point out to other friends when entering that the room was named after me. The only sad part of the story is some years later he further renovated the pub and the Richmond Room got swallowed up and so did the leadlight door. The door would have been perfect at our shack on the river!

Client Impromptu Visits

One of accounting practice clients' biggest or most regular grizzles is that they don't hear from their accountant. I have some defence for accountants in this area, which I cover in my free report *7 Biggest Mistakes Business Owners Make With Their Accountant & How to Turn Their Fees into an Investment.*[*]

Sometimes it is in fact the client's fault that they don't

---

[*] See Appendix B.

hear from their accountant because they don't go out of their way to keep the accountant informed. However, we decided that we would take the initiative and try and be more in our clients' faces. As Steve Jobs said, 'Get closer than ever to your customers. So close that you tell them what they need well before they realise it themselves.'

With this in mind, we encouraged our team to drop in unannounced to see clients if they were travelling past their business. Client response was always very positive and quite often we would win an assignment because we happened to be at the right place at the right time.

History will show that time and again the conversation went along these lines:

Geoff: 'Hi Bob, I was in the area and thought I would drop in and have a coffee if you have time.'

Bob: 'Hey Geoff, sure come in, I've been meaning to call you. I've got a new deal I'm looking to put together that I wouldn't mind you having a look at.'

The five-minute coffee turned into a forty-five-minute discussion about a new deal and a new assignment that eventuated into a new Value Pricing Agreement. Even if it didn't convert into an assignment and was only a forty-five-minute chat, the goodwill created was probably worth more than the fee we generated on other occasions.

We even had this listed on our team KPIs I referred to earlier to measure how often we were doing it.

Just Give Them a Call

Impromptu visits are very impressive to clients but an easier alternative to help keep them engaged is to simply give them a call. All you need to say is, 'How's it going?' Then shut up!

Most clients love to talk about their wins or their

problems. I often believe the best conversationalists are those that say very little but ask the right questions.

If they have a problem, guess what, you have a solution, which turns into an assignment. If they are having some wins, that sounds like a need for some tax planning. If you achieve nothing but a 'Thanks for the call!' you have achieved a lot in terms of client engagement.

Remember, the driving goal is not to pick up business; it is to service clients and help make an impact on their lives. The financial results will flow to you if you achieve the results for your client.

Again, keep a record of impromptu phone calls, not so much to measure of how many but to keep it front of mind and encourage your team to tick the box at least once per month.

Dealing with Complaints

Bill Gates said, 'Your most unhappy customers are your greatest source of learning.'

I learnt a long time ago that a complaint was an opportunity to impress someone. The Net Promoter Score[†] is a test whereby people are surveyed as to their likelihood of referring your business to a friend or colleague. The results are broken into three groups. Those that rate this likelihood between 1-6 are Detractors. Those that rate this likelihood between 7-8 are Passives, and those that rate this likelihood between 9-10 are Promoters.

[†] The Net Promoter Score is a customer loyalty metric developed by (and a registered trademark of) Fred Reichheld and Satmetrix.

The Detractors and the Promoters are the most important groups as they are more likely to tell someone something. Whereas the 7-8 Passives just take things in their stride and don't get excited about too much so will never sing your praises even if they are really happy. These are quite often loyal clients but not necessarily *engaged*.

The Promoters are obvious and we should continue to fuel their enthusiasm, whereas the Detractors are the problem group we need to address. Because they have identified a negative attitude, it means they have an opinion that they are likely to spread. If you can find out what you would need to do to make them raise your score closer to 10, you have a chance of turning a Detractor into a Promoter.

Just like this survey or test, complaints also give you an opportunity to turn a complaint into a positive. Think of the times when you have returned something to a store because it doesn't do what you thought it should do, or it doesn't work at all. As you approach the counter, you could rightly be thinking how this sales assistant is going to try and weasel out of giving a refund.

How different is your experience when the sales assistant says words to the effect, 'I'm so sorry. This is quite unusual for this product. Can I give you a replacement, or would you prefer to receive a cash refund?'

The feeling is that they're on your side immediately. Then imagine if the sales assistant then suggests that they have another model that is a little bit more expensive but will definitely do what you need. In fact, they even go so far as to offer you a discount to buy the improved product as an apology for the inconvenience caused.

In all likelihood, they would probably gain an extra sale from you, a Detractor who marched in through the door intent on demanding a refund, and sent you on your way as a Promotor. What's more, they've gained more profit in their pocket.

Believe it or not, the same happens in a client relationship in an accounting practice. Let's face it, we all make a mess sometimes, but if we hide from the fact or brush it away we can turn Promotors into Passives or even Detractors, and Passives into Detractors. On the other hand, if you fix the problem and even refund the fee you charged them in the first place, they can form the conclusion they are in front and you are a hero.

Every business owner knows that a happy customer tells one or two people whereas an unhappy one tells ten. By going out of your way to deal with complaints, you will increase the rate of spreading the word from happy customers from one or two to four or five, simply because you did something they did not expect.

This raises the issue of accountants being salespeople. Very few people like to be considered salespeople, yet alone professionals who spent hours studying and have earned so much experience as a qualified accountant, lawyer, architect, engineer and so forth. The cold hard fact is that we are acting as sales people day in day out whether we realise it or not. Every interaction with another team member involves one party selling a concept or idea to the other. If they don't buy-in, then you are not going to progress.

It's no different every time you are dealing with a client. You are usually trying to convey some advice to them. If they don't understand or believe your logic, you are not going to serve them to the best degree possible. If you genuinely believe you have a strategy that will give them benefits way in excess of the fee they will invest with you, then you are derelict in your duty for not doing your best to sell that concept to them. What's more, if you do not genuinely believe it's in their best interest, you are a crook for trying to sell it to them!

I was fortunate enough to be given a magnum of Black Label Wolf Blass wine for a birthday present in 1995. The next morning after my birthday party I was admiring my wine and noticed the cork was weeping—not a good sign for a premium bottle of wine. I immediately called the winery to ask what they could do to help. They checked and came back to me to say they didn't have any more of that vintage to top up my bottle and re-cork it, and suggested that I drink it soon. They added, 'By the way, can you give me your name and address? We would like to send you something to compensate you for your inconvenience.'

The following week I received three bottles of wine in the post, one black label, one grey label and one yellow label! Do you think I've told that story a few times? Great PR!

Christmas Functions

A waste of money? No way!

From early on at 2IC Management, we decided to celebrate each year with our clients and it was one of the best marketing spends we did. We literally heeded the advice of Jeff Bezos, CEO of Amazon, when he said, 'We see our customers as invited guests to a party, and we are the hosts. It's our job every day to make every important aspect of the customer experience a little bit better.'

The number of clients who made a point of ensuring

they could make it to our Christmas function was always humbling. Many got to meet other clients who they did not previously know and struck up relationships that still exist today. These functions were not stuffy affairs with speeches and everybody on best behaviour. In fact, I only remember one speech I gave after being hauled out the front of the crowd by one particular client. The speech was not memorable but the act of pulling me out the front was. It was like a sign from this particular client of their way of saying thank you and putting me on the pedestal for everybody to clap.

These functions were initially billed as a 6:30 pm start with an 8:30 pm finish. After the first couple went well into the night we gave up putting a closing time and relied on the establishment we were in telling us to go home. Sometimes this meant the stayers would flow straight into the nearest hotel still open.

Birthday Messages

This is only a small thing, but coming from your accountant is a nice touch.

There are automated Client Relationship Management (CRM) programs that remind you of upcoming birthdays and prompt you to send their template happy birthday message. This also alerts you to wish them happy birthday if you happen to be talking with them.

Happy 29th February!

Many firms send out the stereotype Christmas cards which can have some effect but it doesn't stand out from all the stack of cards a client might receive in the post from all their other suppliers and service providers.

As mentioned earlier, we thought about this and realised that most people start packing away their Christmas cards in mid- to late- January. We came up with the WOW idea to send our clients instead a 'Happy 29th February' card, even when it wasn't a leap year. (I have actually lost count of how many clients responded with, 'This year isn't a leap year!') The point is, we were noticed and our card was very personalised, including team head shots that our team used to create caricatures involved in whatever sport, hobby or passion the particular person was interested in.

The wording also said:[‡] 'We know you have received lots of Christmas Cards and as you have probably packed them away by now we wanted to send you something special from the team at 2IC.'

Menu of Services

Most accountants miss out on fees or upsell because their clients do not fully grasp what they can do for them.

I have had countless discussions with accountants who have regretted one or more of their clients using the services of a consultant or bank manager when they could have helped the client better and cheaper. Yet accountants only

---

[‡] See Appendix F.

have themselves to blame if their clients are not aware of all the services they, as their accountant, can offer.

Clients know accountants prepare tax returns and financial statements; they only have to look at all the advertising signs around suburban practices listing Tax Returns, BAS Returns, Financial Statements, and Bookkeeping. These services are what people expect accountants to do for them. In fact, it's so well known that perhaps accounting firms don't even need to advertise these services.

However, here's a list of what clients probably don't know accounting firms can help with:

- Helping your business grow.
- Solving your day-to-day business problems.
- Helping prepare your business for sale or retirement.
- Advising on staffing problems.

The problem is, if clients don't know how you can help then they won't ask you; they'll ask someone else, perhaps a lawyer.

By developing a Menu of Services and providing it in your welcome pack or available for everyone to see in reception, even your website, you will ensure clients that need help in these particular matters will call on you.

At 2IC Management we made it a point that clients should use us for any business-related problem; if we didn't have the experience or expertise to personally help, we would know or find someone who would.

Client Surveys

Another way of ensuring clients don't feel that you are indifferent to them is to *ask them*. Ask for feedback on what you have done well and, more importantly, what has been received as not so well.

It is much better to find out what you did wrong and then fix it (see my earlier comments in *Dealing With Complaints*) than to get an ethical letter[§] from your competitors. Too often we tend to bury our head in the sand when we know we have messed up, usually out of fear of confrontation. 'Let's hope it will wash over,' we think.

Again, if you hope it washes over, you miss the opportunity to convert a disgruntled client to a raving fan. Furthermore, in all likelihood, even if it does wash over there will always be a scar your business has to carry.

At 2IC Management we sent out surveys on a semi-regular basis.[ʼ] There can be such a thing as too much emphasis on the positive, so we focussed on varying the content of the survey and the timing at which we sent them to our clients. We found that regular six-monthly surveys became monotonous and feedback waned.

We also sent a feedback form on every set of tax returns that went out, which gave clients an opportunity to vent if they weren't happy.

Another opportunity to solve problems!

[§] An ethical letter is a process accounting firms use to notify another firm they have been approached to handle a client's future work.
[ʼ] See an example of one of our surveys at Appendix A.

Client Advisory Boards

We discovered the process of Client Advisory Boards (CABs) from our Results / Principa membership. CABs are very similar to a focus group for marketing surveys. One of the best examples of client advisory was that of a famous entrepreneur in the Unites States who ran a milking dairy. Stew Leonard's dairy went from being a primary production farm to an outlet for milk to a supermarket to eventually a tourist attraction.

One of the key strategies in developing the business was to hold focus group meetings with customers. They would invite customers in to tell them what they didn't like and what they wanted that Stew didn't have.

It is surprising how willing and even keen clients are to provide their opinions if approached. It gives them a level of importance and everyone likes to know their opinion is being acted upon.

Some anecdotes I learned from Stew Leonard's dairy include:

- They received feedback from customers that strawberries at the bottom of the punnets were often squashed and had to be thrown out. Stew introduced large bins of fresh strawberries where people could choose and bag their own, then charged by the gram. As a result, strawberry sales went through the roof because people tended to bag more strawberries at a time than a normal punnet would hold. In addition, Stew started another stall where he sold milkshakes and smoothies made from the squashed strawberries from their bins.

- Stew had a staff incentive strategy that encouraged his team to be cheerful all the time. He didn't want sad faced staff serving his customers. The incentive, or probably more disincentive, was that if you were judged as being a grumpy bum you had to wear the cow suit on a particular day. The cow suit was worn by an individual to walk around the supermarket entertaining the kids and giving away gifts and vouchers.

- Similar to the strawberry effect, Stew had a request for fresh fish. He already supplied fresh fish brought in daily and packaged in sealed containers. However, the customers said they wanted fresh fish displayed on ice so they knew it was fresh. So Stew set up two separate counters, one with the fish as he had always displayed and one with the fish on ice. The results were incredible: with this simple technique, he doubled his fish sales.

At 2IC Management we held a CAB meeting with about eight clients and had it facilitated by a company called RAN ONE.** The feedback was excellent. I was taken aback by how much people were willing to speak their mind in a forum like this when they wouldn't tell you face-to-face. This was even when they knew the meeting was recorded and being sponsored by our business.

One small piece of advice if you are to undertake such a meeting: ensure that whoever facilitates the CAB meeting understands you and your business, and that they have the skills to help with positive reinforcement of your firm.

** RAN ONE was a derivative of RAS.

I can still remember listening to the replay while gardening and cursing at the top of my voice. The moderators from RAN ONE, who as a company were strong promoters of accountants using Fixed Price – Value Pricing Agreements (VPA), allowed one of the participating clients to challenge the concept, which actually got out of hand. They did not offer any counter to his rant by highlighting the obvious benefits that clients received from VPAs, which is something I had to address after the event.

Despite this minor issue, we received a lot of good constructive criticism from the CAB, which we responded directly to the attendees but also used it as another opportunity to build rapport with our full client base. Our letter to clients started with: 'We have been listening to what our clients want...'

Mutual Commitment Statements

It happens surprisingly often that, as accountants, we act in good faith for our clients but the work gets delayed and dragged out. This can happen due to hold-ups beyond our control, but often due to delays or hold-ups on behalf of the client.

I confess, on occasions when it happened, it did irk when some months later the client commented that they weren't happy with the time it took to do their work.

By providing a Mutual Commitment Statement[tt] that is signed off by the client and the accountant, expectations

---

[tt] See Appendix M for a copy of an example of a Mutual Commitment Statement.

from both parties can be agreed to in black and white. It can deal with things like courtesy, timeliness, fees, payment terms, co-operation by clients, and even what the client themselves need to do. It is quite an important document if you are starting an assignment that is out of the normal requirements and where a client's expectations may be vague and unrealistic.

Another benefit we introduced was a commitment by the client to refer others like themselves to us. If they were happy with the services they received, we simply asked them to use their best endeavours to refer someone they might know who could use our services. Incorporating this into the commitment statement became a neat and profitable referral system.

Later in the chapter we will discuss Dr Paddi Lund, but for those who feel uneasy about asking for a referral I will briefly mention Paddi Lund's experience. If they were happy with the outcome, he suggested to his patients to look to refer two new patients to him. However, one patient raised concern with this. Paddi then discovered that the patient was not actually concerned about an obligation to refer friends, rather he was concerned that he was only allowed to refer two.

The problem I have found with most accountants is that they are so busy doing compliance work that they are habitually late in returning calls or meeting clients' deadlines. Why would a client refer someone to you if they are kept waiting for their own work?

The secret is to under promise and overdeliver. A great way to achieve this is to shape your practice using some of the techniques and strategies in this book. Then ask for the referral and see what flows!

Performance Standards

I recently attended a session sponsored by CAANZ (Chartered Accountants Australia and New Zealand) on client engagement. On the agenda was how clients feel more engaged when they know what they are going to get.

A lot of what we did at 2IC Management spawned from team member ideas, RAS/Principa teachings and generally what we thought was a reasonable expectation for clients. As Richard Branson, Founder of the Virgin Group, said, 'The key is to set realistic customer expectations, and then not to just meet them, but to exceed them—preferably in unexpected and helpful ways.'

We therefore had our team design our performance standards. These performance standards were printed on the menu we offered all visitors when they arrived in reception[‡‡], and had things like:

- Answer the phone within three rings.
- Return messages by midday the following day.
- Calling ahead on your behalf to your next appointment if you are running late.

A common theme flowing through this book is the importance of concentrating on people. I've also talked a lot about engagement, something that was bred into me from the beginning at Sims Richmond. For instance, one small thing we insisted all team members do was, whenever they

---

[‡‡] See *Client WOW Ideas* in Chapter 3.

encountered a client in reception or walking to or from an office, to make eye contact and say hello with that client. Whether the client knew them or not was irrelevant.

I didn't think of it as engagement at the time but, I'm absolutely sure the actions of my team helped to build strong client engagement. It wasn't until I attended a session at the CAANZ Conference on client engagement that I realised that this is what I had been doing all along. The presenter highlighted several factors that built client engagement and as I ticked off the list I realised that, yes, we did many of the things suggested and maybe why we were also pretty good at it.[§§]

Guarantees

I am a strong believer in offering guarantees for the service you offer as it sets you apart from the competition. At 2IC Management, we always offered guarantees of our service as well as advising clients to do the same with their services.

It's understandable, but too often business owners are worried about being taken advantage of by customers and clients claiming unwarranted guarantees. This feeling is justified in businesses that deal with customers just once or very rarely. However, the majority of people are honest and believe in doing the right thing.

Yet, for the occasional 'crook' who tries to take advantage of your generosity, you can either:

1. Honour your guarantee and pledge never to do business with them again.

[§§] See *What is Engagement?* in Chapter 4.

2. Challenge their rights to claiming the guarantee.[55] The chances are, if they are being dishonest, they will be disinclined to have an argument or tell others what they've done.

3. The preferred option is to negotiate with them and devise a solution where they feel satisfied and you retain a customer for life.

Now let's look at the chances of this happening with your accounting clients. We are all looking for more customers 'of the type we like'. The chances are the type we like will not be trying to take advantage of us. For the clients you have had for some time, you will hopefully have built a trusted relationship with them and thus minimise the chances of them ripping you off.

The other factor to ask yourself is: 'What would you do if such and such went wrong?' More often than not, when I ask that same question to my accounting or consulting clients, the answer will be: 'We would fix it, pay for it or do it again.' So why not guarantee it if you already know you will cop the loss?

Highlighting what you already know you will do if something went wrong and offering it as a guarantee sets you apart from others. For instance, most accountants would pay for any late lodgement penalties to the ATO that their clients may incur if it was the accountants fault. Guaranteeing this will give comfort to your client and build trust.

A client once told me that one of the special features we provided that he valued was tax audit insurance. 2IC Management were early adopters in this field, but the client

---

[55] A word of note: be careful because, as we've already discussed, an unhappy customer tells ten times as many people as a happy customer.

clearly felt comfort in having this arranged for him. Essentially, he was guaranteed that he would not have to pay any additional fees if he were to be singled out by the ATO for an audit.

Guarantees also work particularly well with value pricing proposals. When you are fixing a price upfront with the value in the client's eye, a guarantee helps comfort the client that they will receive exactly what they expect.

From a client's point of view, your business comes from a position of strength when your advice on a particular strategy tailored for them is backed up with a fixed investment and a guarantee of the outcomes that you control. Guarantees are not a gimmick. You are not trying to coerce someone into buying something they don't need by offering a guarantee; you are simply taking the risk out of their decision by backing your own confidence in what you can do for them.

Obviously, in the accounting and business consulting environment you cannot always guarantee outcomes, as these are quite often outside your control. What you can guarantee, however, are the outcomes inside your control. It goes without saying that if it's within your control and you are charging for it, your customers should expect to get what they are paying for.

Often, I might use terms like: 'By engaging our services I cannot guarantee the end result but you guarantee yourself the best chance of achieving your desired outcome.' I would then go on to guarantee timelines, milestones and other performance standards.

If by some chance you make mistakes that affect the guarantee of your service, don't wait for the client to claim their guarantee because this can create an awkward position for them. Write the cheque or pay the consequence of your guarantee and get on with it. You'll find that they will often not cash the cheque.***

At 2IC Management, we were very keen to keep our performance at the level we indicated to our clients. In fact, one of the agenda items at our team meetings was to discuss any failures we may have made. If we discovered a breach of standards, we backed it up by sending a letter of apology to the client with a complimentary dinner voucher with one of our restaurant clients.†††

One of the guarantees we have offered in the past goes along these lines: 'If for whatever reason you are not totally satisfied with our performance under our Platinum Service Package, we will refund you the amount of the value you believe you missed out on.' We also pointed out that if we didn't agree with their assessment, we reserved the right to cease providing our services from then on.

Value Pricing

Imagine calling an airline and asking how much will it cost for a flight to Sydney. What would your response be if the consultant said something like: 'Well, we can't really tell you at this stage. We don't know whether the airport will be fogged in at that time of day or how many people will be boarding, which may take longer, so we're now introducing a charge by the hour service.'

*** Even with the availability of online banking and EFT, I still advise the use of cheques because some clients won't cash them. What's important is the offer of reimbursing them.
††† See Appendix S for a sample of this letter.

Doesn't make a lot of sense, does it? So why do so many professionals claim the right to charge by the hour? Who should get paid more for being inefficient? What gives Accountant A the right to charge $500 per hour while Accountant B charges $200?

Many other service industries have moved away from hourly rate charges for regular type work, such as dentists, builders and even motor mechanics. Accountants seem to fret about not getting paid for every hour their team works on a job, regardless of the value they bring to the client. Let's face it, preparing financial statements and tax returns is a process workers role and a fixed fee should be able to be set for this process.

The other factor that supports a fixed fee is the fact that the majority of firms will examine their WIP at the end of the job, see what they charged last year and then decide whether they can push the price a bit or whether they need to discount it regardless of the WIP. Unfortunately, rather than trying to assess the value, the same practitioner will often only charge what is on the WIP if it is lower than last year. This is where many accountants have undersold the value they have provided over the years. Furthermore, the whole process is only going to get trickier with the introduction of the cloud-based software and outsourcing.

I have been an eager student of value pricing for some time and friends like Ron Baker and Ric Payne have regularly highlighted the flaws of time-based billing. Ric in particular has pointed out that on a retrospective examination of the development of accounting practice, all efficiencies have constantly been passed onto the client.

When I started my accounting apprenticeship, we didn't have computers to prepare financials. We had manual cashbooks and Multiple Column Trial Balance Sheets. Long and laborious work, to say the least. Just as I explained the drawn-out process to enter time sheets and the reconciliation of WIP and Debtors at my first job at Harris & Orchard, the process of doing manual financial statements will be foreign to most accountants today. Rather than posting to a software program, all cheques were entered into a multiple column cashbook and dissected under various headings to identify the type of expense or capital purchase. These cashbooks would often be ten to fifty pages long depending on the size of the business. All the columns were then added for the period of the financial statements and cross added to a control total.

A similar process was then done for bankings, then posted to a general ledger book or worksheet. Manual journal entries were also entered and all general ledgers were added and reconciled to ensure they balanced. A job that may take a day using cloud technology today could well have taken weeks to do manually.

Then along came computers and we are able to code straight to ledgers and save countless hours. But despite such greater efficiencies, the accounting profession kept charging by the hour as they had done previously.[‡‡‡] Even though they increased their hourly rates since then, these rates were usually tied to the remuneration being paid to the particular employee and the partners, who were paid a bit higher because of their roles and responsibilities.

The end result is, as Ric Payne observed, we passed all the efficiencies gained with modern technology onto the clients.

[‡‡‡] In the earlier days, we did actually have a charge rate for the use of the computer because most of the processing was performed by specialist employees. Once we all had our own PCs, the charge rate for computers disappeared.

This is about to happen again in a big way as firms look to compete with discount offerings and ever-advancing software. This is totally reasonable. If you can't offer the same product or service at the same or better price, you will lose the business. Accounting firms just offering process worker services will need to develop a pretty slick model that works because the current one is stuck in turn of the millennia processes and won't keep up with the future model for most firms.

However, it's not all doom and gloom. If your firm is able to position its services on a value basis, then you can charge as a Knowledge Worker. The ideal is to be paid for the results we achieve. Whether the service or solution takes us one hour or one minute, the consumer shouldn't care, as long as they have the outcome they approached you for.

I have had a number of arguments with lawyers about the value based pricing model. They go something like this:

> Let's say a new client approaches an accountant, or for that matter a lawyer, with quite a complex matter. The professional uses his knowledge and decades of experience to work through the minefields to create a solution. Typically, the professional will look at their WIP to see how much time they have spent, possibly lick their finger and put it up to the wind to determine whether they will mark up or write down the WIP. Let's say the client is absolutely rapt with the outcome and is very happy to pay the fee.
>
> Now let's assume another client comes from nowhere with a very similar problem. The professional now probably needs far less time and

> *resources to do the job. The question now becomes, what should they charge?*

I, together with other value pricing enthusiasts, believe the fee should be quoted based on the value that can be provided to the client. This may mean the same job will be worth more to one client than the next, and why not? This is a very important concept to master when entering the regime of value pricing. Under no circumstances am I suggesting a solution for a first client that was costed and priced at $X should be the same for the next client. That is not a representation of value because value is 'in the eye of the beholder'. I maintain the next client could get a lower price on the same service if it does not represent the same value to them. Conversely, if the value created by your knowledge, experience and efforts is higher, then the second client should invest in a higher fee. Let's also remember that in today's litigious society, if something goes wrong and the client suffers in part because of the advice you have given them, you will be staring at possible damages for the value lost, not the fee charged, and probably more.

The benefits of Value Pricing for clients are:

1. They have certainty of how much they are choosing to invest before they make the decision.
2. They can decide to go forward with the assignment knowing the investment.
3. Once a fee is established, the professional and the client can agree to a payment plan that can help spread the payments over a period of time rather than receive a one-off bill due for payment within 30 days.

The benefits of value pricing for the professional are:

1. They have certainty of how much remuneration they are choosing to work for before they make the decision.
2. The client is much more likely to accept a fee proposal before the assignment commences because they are keen to reach the desired outcome. Given most outcomes are not guaranteed, the client will often be looking at the optimistic outcome or, alternatively, if they look at the pessimistic outcome, they know their exposure to weigh up against the investment in your services. Compare this to raising a fee after the event. If it is a good outcome, the client is often only focussed on their result and can lose track of the contribution you made. Worse, if there is an unfavourable outcome, the client will place little or no value on your hard toil.
3. It enables the practice to get paid either before or while the assignment is being carried out. This assists with lockup issues compared to raising fees after the event then waiting 30, 60 or even 90 days to get paid.
4. Once you know all the compliance jobs you have scheduled for a year, it's very easy to budget for the financial results of the business. You will also know your overheads, so then the only variable will be one-off assignments or new clients. The marginal income from these variables then becomes net profit straight to your bottom line. This means there is no need to achieve an hourly

rate for this extra income and value pricing becomes a much easier concept to accept and implement.

What's more, clients don't want to buy your time. Your clients are happy to invest in other things like:

- Results.
- Expectations.
- Good Feelings.
- Hope.
- Dreams.
- A preferred vision of the future.
- Integrity.
- Honesty.
- Solutions to problems.
- And even the relationships that foster all or some of the above.

Time Sheets

In my opinion, time sheets are a means of measuring performance of your team if you do not have any other systems to do so.

In 2006, I followed the lead of VPA purists and launched a campaign of Tear Up Your Time Sheets (see Chapter 3, *Tear Up Your Time Sheets*). We held a special function with clients where we not only wined and dined them but made a big deal about the Value Pricing Agreements we were about to launch. At the function, I presented a summary on the benefits to clients of VPAs and also used the occasion to showcase my team. It was a very successful function and it paved the way for our introduction of VPAs.

The system of no time sheets worked well for 2IC Management while I had a team that were focussed on providing value. However, I do admit there were times where it did break down for me. With hindsight, I would have done it differently. One of my biggest failings was to put the trust I expect people to give me into people I deal with, whether that was team members, clients or other business associates. I've paid dearly a few times, but I put it down to lessons learned in the long run and advice I can pass onto others.

My problems arose with the process worker issues, not the Knowledge Worker VPAs. Without time sheets, I had no measure as to how much time some team members were spending on compliance work and I failed to implement systems to measure this. There are some who advocate time sheets with $1 units for all team members to monitor productivity. I see this as counterproductive as, if you are going to go to the trouble of recording it, you may as well allocate a rate that reflects the value that the various team members should be able to provide.

I re-introduced time sheets after deciding to sell my practice as the most conventional recording to present to a potential buyer. However, if I was running an accounting practice now, I would be setting the fee before each compliance job and then letting each team member know how much production they are expected to make towards various key performance drivers they will be involved in. Whether this is recorded via time sheets or some other method would depend on the type of practice.

Dr Paddi Lund

From my early exposure to RAS, Paul Dunn introduced us to a very weird but successful character named Dr Paddi Lund. Paddi was a dentist that had reinvented his practice and his strategies have helped shape what I was able to do at 2IC Management.

Paddi had a practice where the only patients he would see were those that were referred to him by patients who *earned the right* to refer. Paddi had the most amazing referral program.

In his program, he would offer his patients a referral card that they could hand to a close friend who would appreciate the type of offerings he provided. He also had a Mutual Commitment Statement whereby clients committed to refer at least two clients per year. He ventured down this path with a degree of caution as to whether he would offend patients by this request. As previously discussed earlier in this chapter, he encountered an initial problem, or what he thought was a problem. One patient became coy in their response and Paddi was quite worried that he may have pushed his marketing too hard in the traditionally, conservative profession of dentistry. It turned out the patient's only concern was that he was only allowed to refer two friends and not more. From there the floodgates opened!

Other non-traditional strategies implemented by Paddi Lund were:

- He introduced a very different reception to traditional dentists:

- There was no sign on the front of his building to indicate there was a dental practice in existence. The front door was locked and only booked patients were allowed entry. He displayed a very large barista coffee machine in reception and his reception team would daily bake cakes to be served to patients while they waited. He had a large range of teas and served tea or coffee in quality fine china.

- Each patient would be led to a special waiting room with their name on the door where they would be served their selected tea, coffee, cake or whatever to eventually be met by Paddi to discuss their treatment.

- His dental theatre was a trailblazer to current standards where he mounted bulky TVs from the ceiling for patients to watch (way before flat screen TVs were released).

- He worked significantly less hours and earned significantly higher net income than his peers. This was not based on simply charging a higher rate but providing a more detailed service and offering higher quality products and services.

- He established a referral system whereby he re-ferred patients to his competitors when they did not fit the mould of the type of patient he wished to service. This was a major influence on my decision to cull my client base and find a different firm for some that did not fit the mould for our services. Paddi Lund was an ard-ent follower of Paul Dunn and unlike many business owners, or for that matter accounting principals, he took up the challenge and was happy to implement ideas Paul suggested. Paddi however, took things to the next level.

Paddi Lund went on to write several books, which I recommend any serious client service provider should read.[§§§] In his books he identified what he has labelled Critical Non-Essentials or CNEs. Basically, Paddi came to realise that people value what you do for them not necessarily by the quality of the professional services you provide. They put more value on the other little things that they witness during their interaction with you than anything else. In other words, do the little things right and they will have confidence that you will do the big things right.

Think of when you go to your doctor for a check-up or because you're feeling unwell. How do you really know whether the doctor is giving you correct advice or proper diagnosis? We tend to trust that they will get it right. Similarly, most of your clients do not know whether you have balanced their books correctly or provided them with the best tax outcomes. I'm also sure many accountants can vouch how often they have picked up a new client's books and seen how a previous accountant did not deserve the trust bestowed on them by their client.

One story Paddi Lund tells that always stays with me is about a plumber who won an award for the best plumber in a region. He was on his way to the award ceremony dressed in his tuxedo when he received a call for a job, which happened to be on the way to the ceremony. The elderly lady seemed quite distressed so he decided he would pop in on the way and help. Needless to say, the old lady was surprised to see

---

[§§§] See Bibliography.

a plumber at her door in a tuxedo, but very happy when he fixed her problem.

The following week the plumber got a number of calls from residents near the old lady. It seemed she was so happy with his efforts she spread the word. When he arrived at the first home, he was greeted by another elderly citizen but with a noticeable look of disappointment on her face. Eventually the plumber realised they were all expecting him to roll up in his tuxedo.

I'm not even sure that Paddi's story is factual, but it gets the message across. It's the little things that are going to impress your clients. The plumber's clients didn't know whether he was good at what he did, but they wanted his service. Likewise, most accountants' clients don't know if their accountants are any good, but it's the little things that keeps them coming back and even referring you to other clients.

Here are some of the little things that will help build trust in the eyes of your clients:

- Getting their names correct.
- Posting to the correct address.
- Correct spelling and grammar.
- Neatly presented offices.
- Lodging on time.
- Returning their calls promptly.
- Properly formatted financial statements.

The list goes on and on, but the one common thing with all the above items is that none of these little things require an accounting degree. Furthermore, clients certainly have the know-how to detect if you get them right. But how often do we see them not up to standard?

WOW Packs

Although amongst ourselves we referred to them as WOW Packs, as that was their primary purpose, to our clients we labelled them as Welcome Packs.

A Welcome Pack was a means of setting the scene for our new clients to know what their expectations of us could be. At 2IC Management, this was one of the key features in building rapport and client engagement.

Typically, our Welcome Packs had:

- Contact details.
- Details of how to get to our office.
- Opening office hours.
- A Menu of Services.
- Mutual Commitment Statements (including a referral commitment from your client).
- Fee arrangements.
- Mission Statement.
- Performance Standards.
- Reception Menu.

You can include anything else specific to your business and service that you consider will WOW your client.

Paul O'Byrne

I could not write this book without mentioning a person

who I did not know all that well, having met him only a few times, but who certainly had a big influence on my business and life.

Paul O'Byrne was a founding partner in a firm in the UK called O'Byrne & Kennedy (OBK).''' Paul taught me the principal of sacking clients. OBK went from five hundred clients to fifty and significantly increased their profits.

I recall a BFO moment whilst listening to Paul deliver a presentation on this topic of sacking clients. Sometime before, I had followed his doctrine and sacked a bunch of clients. Not that I didn't like them; in fact, I found it very hard to tell close friends that I would not do their work anymore. It was more that I had chosen a career that did not include their type of work anymore. It's just as if you were to utilise the services of a friend who worked at a particular business who then resigned to embark on a different career. You may be disappointed that they could not help you anymore, but you wouldn't hold a grudge, and neither did my friends.

I was able to bundle up the selected clients and refer them to another firm. This process turned out to be a win-win-win. I received payment for goodwill from the firm receiving my referrals, that firm received new clients at a price he was willing to pay to grow his business, and the client was not left stranded with nobody to help them out.

In the twelve months leading up to my BFO, I had been convinced to buy into a practice, which went totally against my new philosophy of sacking unsuitable clients. I still went ahead with the venture, however, even though I knew taking on more clients would diminish my ability to grow services

---

''' I recommend that you view their website at: www.obk.co.uk. From this you will get to understand a bit about the character of the late Paul O'Byrne who passed away in 2008 and also about the legacy he created with his partner Paul Kennedy.

to existing customers. What was I thinking? I remember sitting in the front row of the conference as Paul was delivering his presentation and sinking into my seat feeling stupid. Here I was, having purchased a practice full of the type of clients I had previously sacked!

My BFO made, I rushed straight back to my office and set in motion a means to bundle up new clients and sell them to several practices I knew were interested in buying the type of fees I didn't want. Again, a win-win-win.

OBK had some other very interesting innovations that we used for our R&D:

- They developed their own MBA accreditation where clients would attend a course that would eventually result in a graduation ceremony.
- They had each member of their team identified on their website with headshots of famous actors and actresses.****
- They created some very funny videos as a testimonial for Ric Payne at Principa, which again got a serious message across in a very fun way.
- They developed a reputation of an employer of choice where accountants would approach them for a job and agree to a drop in wages to what they were receiving at their current employment. How many firms can claim this accolade?
- They were trailblazers in trashing time sheets and developed a method of measuring team performance without time sheets.
- All their fees were based on value pricing and

**** This has now been removed. I'm not sure if it was due to unauthorised usage of the photos or something else, but for me it certainly made a statement about the fun attitude they had at OBK.

Paul O'Byrne consulted internationally to professional firms on the implementation of value pricing.

Thank you, Paul, you were not with us long enough but you made a huge impact on a lot of people and businesses.

Do they Fog a Mirror?

There's a joke in accounting circles about the concept of what is a desirable client. If they can fog a mirror they are suitable; if not, there is an opportunity for estate planning and succession planning work.

Most firms will take on an interview with a new prospective client and not set parameters as to whether they are the type of client they want to do business with. We developed criteria for interviewing new clients and we told them what they were at their first interview. We did not want to deal with anyone who simply wanted us to prepare their tax returns and financial statements and see us once a year. We also explained that we did not take on a client unless we expected their fees would grow to at least $10,000 per annum. I would go on to explain that because we priced our services on value they should be happy to pay us as much as we can generate because they would derive a multiple on our fees as a return on their investment.

I would always preface this initial interview with questions as to why they were changing accountants. Whenever fees were raised I drilled down, and clients *always* confirmed it wasn't about the fee itself but the value they believed they got for it. Unfortunately, a compliance accountant will always have difficulty persuading their client of the value of preparing tax returns and financial statements.

A, B and C Class Clients

As I mentioned in my comments about Paul O'Byrne, there is a strong argument for classifying clients into different classes. Whether that be A, B and C or some other classing that suits your model.

We looked at our C-class clients (and this had nothing to do with their character, as I mentioned they were often good personal friends) and advised them we were no longer doing work in the area that they needed assistance. We also offered them assistance by identifying where they could go to get what they needed; usually a personal tax return or a once a year investment tax return.

It's interesting that we actually had some of these 'sacked clients' refer colleagues to us for more consulting type assistance. This highlights that by educating your clients about what you 'don't do' they became aware of what you 'do do', and because we had a good relationship, even though it had ended, they became a quality referrer.

Set Your Own Criteria that Suits You

You don't have to follow the lines we did at 2IC Management

or any of Paul O'Byrne's methods, but I'm sure you have clients that you don't really enjoy working with or your team don't enjoy.

I've had some frank phone calls with grumpy clients telling them that if they were going to talk to my team the way they did then I wouldn't be doing business with them. I would much rather lose a client who was a pain than to have a key team member leave through having to deal with the wrong kind of clientele. As I have mentioned earlier, my team is more important in the long-term than any specific client.

What is Engagement?

I attended a session at the Chartered Accountants Australia & New Zealand Business Forum in 2015, *The Five Service Elements to Creating Client Engagement… and Driving Profit, Advocacy and Cross-sell* delivered by David King, Managing Director of Vue Consulting.

I was interested in the key elements to successfully engage clients, as I believe all businesses should be. I was pleasantly surprised by what I learned. Here are some take-home points from the session:

The Benefits of Client Engagement

David King divided the client base into four quadrants: Engaged, Complacent, Content, and Disgruntled.

Several of the tables he presented from his research showed the benefits of client engagement:

	% Highly Satisfied	% Highly Loyal
Engaged	90%	99%
Complacent	82%	97%

	% Provided Referral	% Provided Feedback
Engaged	100%	74%
Complacent	0%	55%

David highlighted that the major benefit of client engagement is turning them into brand advocates. The more engaged they are, the more loyal they are and the more likely they are to refer your business and provide feedback.

Furthermore, another overwhelming statistic provided in this session was that engaged clients contribute significantly more to revenue, profit share and advocacy than contented, complacent or disgruntled clients.

What is More Engaging for Clients?

During the presentation, David posed a number of questions and suggested answers:

1. What is more engaging to clients?
    - A. Defined Service Levels
    - B. Good Support Team
    - C. Speed: Emails/Calls Returned

    Answer: A. Defined Service Levels.

Because it makes service standards tangible, visual and clear. It encourages client questions and ensures they understand your levels of service, as well as managing their expectations from the start.

2. What is more engaging to clients?

    A.   Problems Resolved Quickly
    B.   Strong Personal Relationship
    C.   Good Range of Services

Answer: B. Strong Personal Relationship.

This can be achieved by leading the way and sharing first on difficult topics and not making assumptions—always ask. To build a strong personal relationship you need to earn the right to ask the tough, open questions.

3. What is more engaging to clients?

    A.   Receiving Clear Reports
    B.   Accurate Client Records
    C.   Clear Explanations

Answer: C. Clear Explanations.

David suggested sending pre-meeting materials to help clients prepare, use collaborative in-meeting agendas and send (short and prompt) post-discussion summaries.

4. What is more engaging to clients?

    A.   Reliable Professional
    B.   Proactive Professional
    C.   Access to external Professionals

Answer: B. Proactive Professional.

Tips are to use a rolling 'next meeting' strategy for 'A' Clients, create a 'batch review' process for 'B' Clients, and use a client discussion preparation tool.

5. What is more engaging to clients?

    A. Client's Business is Valued

    B. Trustworthy Professional

    C. Uniqueness of Advice

Answer: A. Client's Business is Valued.

Some ways to make clients feel their business is valued are: to ask them for their advice on something; involving them in your business decisions; and celebrating their anniversaries.

Many accountants might choose some of the answers to the questions above that relate to core offerings or traits that clients just expect from an accounting firm. However, the answers that build engagement are *what make you different from the rest.*

~5~

Time & Profit

'Time management is an oxymoron. Time is beyond our control, and the clock keeps ticking regardless of how we lead our lives. Priority management is the answer to maximising the time we have.'

John C. Maxwell

Working Hours and Leave

In the early days at Sims Richmond, I worked long hours but always kept weekends to myself. This didn't always relate to more family time, as Gerry would attest, as I continued to play Aussie Rules football until my early thirties and then coached for a few years after that.[*]

I did take regular holiday leave, but in my partnership with Dennis Sims I did it with a degree of guilt because he just worked himself so hard. I probably averaged four weeks leave per year in my fifteen-year partnership with Dennis. When I turned fifty, however, I justified to myself that I was entitled to long service leave, having been in practice for twenty-seven years. I did the sums and worked out that with accrued long service leave and with it continuing to accrue I could take ten weeks leave a year for a decade and only be drawing what I am entitled to (that is, four weeks' annual leave per year and long service leave continuing to accrue).

On reflection, I wonder why I needed to justify anything. Why shouldn't this be the plan for a successful business owner? If you are doing the right thing and creating the right results for clients and your team, you should decide what your rewards are.

I'm not suggesting all practitioners should take ten weeks leave, some would prefer four weeks' quality time off in a five-star resort, whereas I am more budget conscious on holidays and am more than happy to relax on an affordable vacation in Bali. The important message, however, is that I was able to take the time off and the practice did not suffer

---

[*] Refer to my biggest mistake *Ignoring Work-Life Balance* in Chapter 2 and how you can't get back lost time with your family.

for my absence. As pointed out in Chapter 3, *It's the End of the World as We Know It!*, when I had my major health issue, I was also able to take sick leave for three months full-time and a further three months part-time.

The key to having time off was the combination of delegation and systems. I have dealt with delegation in detail earlier in Chapter 3, *Delegation*, but it is such an important ingredient to building your team, creating extra time and growing your practice that I felt it necessary to mention it again. Furthermore, creating systems, together with empowering the right people to implement them, meant I had time for creating ideas to improve what we did as a business and to take leave when I wanted to.

I believe nobody can work every day for weeks, months, even years on end without burning out. We all need time away. We all need holidays to recharge and relax. Every practitioner should therefore aim to create a business where they can take their desired time off per year and not feel guilty.

If it's part of the plan, you will not feel guilty and you'll enjoy the time off.

Time is not Money... Value IS!

I can remember justifying my fees to clients in the early days that 'Time is Money!' The smarter business people are learning this is just so wrong.

Business owners have the same amount of time to devote to business, so why is it that some end up with more money than others if time equals money? The reason is because some provide more value than others.

Or probably more importantly, they provide more perceived value than others. This is why the BIG 4 accountancy firms can charge twice as much as the suburban accountant to prepare a basic tax return. But why? Is it because of who they are? Is it their reputation?

Not necessarily. It has more to do with the fact that they ask for it! And more importantly, because their clients perceive it as being more valuable. Perception is reality. If a client perceives value in your business, then that's their reality.

When I was younger in practice, I placed a lot more value on accounting skills (probably more accurately described as bookkeeping) than was probably warranted. I even sacked employees who weren't up to the standards we thought appropriate, at the same time overlooking other attributes that were important. The fear, I guess, was not getting sued for making mistakes. But, as with Paddi Lund's Critical Non-Essentials, most of the time clients don't know whether the figures are right or not. What they do know, though, is the relationships they build with people they like, know and trust. In fact, they are actually buying that relationship, not the numbers that are produced in a set of financials.

This emphasises my belief about people and business, and the theme of this book. I know of no better way of building an accounting practice, and for that matter any business, around a core value that is more successful than building relationships with people. More recently at Straight Talk Group, we constantly reinforce to our clients that they are not selling to a company, no matter how big the corporation they are dealing with, they are always selling to a person or to people.

So, what does this mean? The fact is, there are accounting firms that produce substandard financials but have a client base of valued customers who pay for their relationship. And the clients are getting what they paid for!

Recently I helped a Small to Medium Enterprise (SME) with an insolvency issue that highlights this point. This SME had two related entities where, for two years in a row, the balance sheets for each of the entities had inter-entity loan accounts that actually changed during the period. Nothing unusual, except in both entities it showed that the other entity owed it money. Both had assets on their balance sheets that claimed the other entity owed it money and the balances moved in the second year. I shudder to think what the balancing journal must have been like.

The point is, these accountants are getting paid for the perceived value they sell to their clients. In fact, they are selling their relationship; not time, not financial statements.

This is an example of poor quality getting paid for perceived value, which is something as a profession we should not be proud of. However, it highlights the fact that time is not money. I'm not advocating that it's okay to produce substandard financial statements. Rather that the client is in a better position having a good relationship with their accountant helping with their business than dealing with a pure compliance accountant, who may get the financials right but doesn't help the client improve their business.

What I would prefer to highlight is the fact that clients will pay for value add services that provide a return on their investment and not necessarily how long you spend on providing that financial service.[†]

[†] See *Value Pricing*, Chapter 4.

Profit

As accountants, we know the concepts that drive profit, but some attitudes in the profession probably don't reflect a real understanding of what really drives profit.

The adage of Time x Rate Per Hour doesn't work anymore. Below I discuss some of the principles I was able to use to drive my planning.

Budgets and Projections

From year one in practice at Sims Richmond, Dennis and I would create a budget on the year ahead based on the fees we knew we had with our current stable of clients.

This is the first reason why time-based billing is such a false concept—we already knew what we were going to charge the majority of our clients before the year started. We could do this back in 1979 without computer systems, so practices don't need high-end technology to do it today.

We then set a target for growth, what we wanted to win in new business. This gave us a basis for our resource needs for staffing so we would go out and find the appropriate new team member/s.

At this point in time, an accounting firm has little if any variable costs. Back then the biggest variable was probably paper. Therefore, as all our costs were fixed, every additional dollar fee went straight to the bottom line. There was no need to earn a certain hourly rate for every new job secured—$1 per hour for 20 hours added $20 profit!

With this method, we were able to forecast profit by additional income targeted, not by additional hours times an hourly rate.

Benefit of VPAs—Profit is Set with only Upside

This is where value pricing makes budgeting more dynamic.

Once all fixed compliance fees for the year are set, you know the minimum profit you will make because all your expenses are within your control and pretty much fixed. You also don't get a surprise when a particular client fails to bring in their work one year and moves elsewhere. Because you get an agreement early in the year both on the fixed fee and the monthly repayments, these surprises don't tend to happen. If the client is unhappy, this will manifest very early when they refuse to commit to a fee. At worse, you have a chance of converting that unhappy client to a happy one and maybe even the raving fan we are all after.

I would then target an amount of value add work that would flow by natural attraction. This work would also need to be quoted on a VPA basis, but provided you haven't cut your team too fine just to perform compliance work, there is a lot less pressure on how much to charge. Many accountants are very concerned about quoting on this basis because of fears of a write off (usually because it goes down as a black mark when profit bonuses are reviewed).‡

In reality, partners should be welcoming these opportunities to add guaranteed profit to the bottom line. Moreover, quite often one-off projects bring an opportunity to quote at values that will return much higher hourly rates.

More profit for you.

Spare Capacity

‡ The constant pressure on outperforming other partners is highlighted in the story in Chapter 3 about the Big 4 partner flying in an expert from interstate to provide a service that one of the local partners specialised in.

I recently had a client tell me; 'You can't bank margins, but you can bank cash!' Words of wisdom from a hotelier, which I suspect he learned from my years of tutelage. Unfortunately, accountants often overlook this concept. Many partnerships focus on the hourly rate rather than the actual revenue earned. If you have spare capacity, and you should always plan this, why not keep the clients and the team happy by doing extra assignments at a lower hourly rate? The most likely outcome is that, because you have spare capacity, you will be available when opportunity knocks to do extra work. Furthermore, if it provides real value to your client you will earn above average hourly rates. Again, more profit for you.

Once the 'natural attraction one-offs' are costed in, you can be quite aggressive with building new opportunities. This provides super profits and again has no association with hourly rates. Again, I emphasise this is in no way profiteering from clients. Remember, it's all about people and building relationships! You are simply offering an outcome to a client that they are willing to invest in.

At 2IC Management, we would, as a team, brainstorm what we could offer as a service for the coming year and target how many clients we could attract at a standard fee. Sometimes, ideas would surface based on a requested assignment from one particular client or a problem we identified for another client. We were then able to 'widgetize' the solution into an offer for either our whole client base or for a particular sector.

Unless you have spare capacity, however, this will never be possible with any level of commitment.

Leveraged Offerings

At 2IC Management, our team also used and created 'Leveraged Offerings'.

Business Coaching

A firm involved in value add consulting services constantly assists clients in the development of strategies for their business. Many times I have had meetings with clients to plan a strategy that had significant benefits for the client. Then along came FTI—Failure to Implement. All too often, the next time I spoke to the client and asked how the strategy was going, I received the answer, 'We've been so busy I haven't had a chance to do anything about that.'

Practices like 2IC Management give constant advice to clients, only to have them searching for excuses as to why they didn't implement the required strategy. I find this extremely frustrating. All the good work we put in to devise the strategy seems wasted, sometimes forever, because action was required before a certain deadline. At other times it has to be revisited to go over the steps that need implementing.

In reality, most accounting practices also participate in FTI, even myself. Many times I have attended a seminar and had a BFO, then discussed the new idea with colleagues at the conference, thinking how great my business would be once we started doing it. I have even gotten excited and discussed it with my wife and raved about it with partners and team members back in the office. Then some months later I attended a similar seminar and that the same BFO jumped at me again.

'I was going to do that twelve months ago!' I lambast myself, and the cycle starts all over again.

There are many practices that know what needs implementing to improve their life and the lives of their clients and team but something always gets in the way:

- Client crisis.
- ATO deadlines.
- One partner doesn't understand why it needs to be done.
- Pushback from key stakeholders.
- Change is hard to implement.
- We'll do it next year.

The list goes on and on, but just like any business, accounting practices could do with a business coach to hold them accountable and ensure they do not suffer from FTI. In 2010 I was approached by a group operating under the banner of 10X Ltd., a franchise that specialised in business coaching for accounting practices. The concept was perfect, but the model was very flawed. Nonetheless, this spawned my newest business venture, Straight Talk Group. By offering business coaching services, I was then able to assist clients ensure good ideas for their business are implemented.

Business coaching can be provided on a one-on-one basis or in a more leveraged environment via coaching clubs or mastermind sessions. Some practices anoint a particular team member, whether a partner or employee, to provide coaching services. Accountants don't necessarily make great coaches, however, as a coach's role is to help their client explore options and encourage them to do the work and find the solutions. Accountants are always in 'solution mode' and quite often jump into solutions without exploring deep enough to find the actual root of the problem.

At Straight Talk Group, we have engaged a business

coach specifically to deliver these services. We have chosen a team member highly credentialed in both life coaching and business coaching, which enables us to offer a much broader line of advice and direction.

While helping clients to be more successful is the driving purpose of business coaching, another benefit is that the accounting services function invariably increases once clients engage a coach. This is because the client and coach develop ideas that have financial ramifications or may need approaches to financiers or stakeholders. There is less FTI as, after a strategy is decided upon, the coach marches the client into the next room to get the accountant working on the numbers.

In fact, one of the major flaws in the 10X model was this flow-on benefit for the accounting firms. 10X promoted a concept of holding seminars and workshops for clients to introduce them to coaching programs. The accounting firms benefitted simply by raising their clients' expectations on what they could do for them and they became more engaged at the accountant-client level.

The overriding role of the coach is to hold the client accountable to implement the agreed strategies, whether they were devised during the coaching session or from the value add consulting advice from the accountant. Being held accountable for action means no more FTI. The result is that the client has a much bigger win from the strategies that have been developed with them.

Regardless of whether you employ a specialist coach or you take off your accountant's hat and put on a coach's hat, introducing business coaching to any practice has many benefits, including:

- A further means of engaging your clients and turning them into raving fans.
- More profitable clients.[§]
- An additional service to your clients that they will invest in based on value not time.
- Generates extra accounting work from clients who develop ideas with their business coach.
- The ability to corral your clients under your control. Because many coaches form relationships with accountants, you can attract new clients to your firm and prevent current clients from moving to another firm.
- Further revenue streams going to the bottom line not requiring hourly rate considerations.
- A group coaching program that clients can invest in at a lower cost per participant providing a higher return on their investment whilst offering the practice a higher return per hour through the leveraging of group sessions.

As Lisa O., our coach at Straight Talk Group, says, 'A successful mastermind removes business owner isolation and acts as a non-executive board for its members, creates a great learning platform, increased accountability and fabulous networking. The knowledge in the room is leveraged as the sum of the members is way greater than the parts.'[¶]

[§] This is a very key issue. I strongly believe that if you assist clients to become more profitable, the dollars will eventually flow your way either from charging by value rather than time, or by having more demand for your services from current and new clients, or both.

[¶] See Appendix C. Our business coach Lisa O. highlights coaching strategies and some of the wins we have been involved in at Straight Talk Group.

Group Training Sessions

The resources we were provided through the RAS-Principa networks enabled 2IC Management to develop training sessions we could deliver to our clients.

One of the most popular training sessions was educating clients to 'understand the numbers'. We created a workshop called 'Effective Financial Management' that went for a day, sometimes as a one day event but usually as two half days. The workshop educated clients to understand financial statements and focused on the basics, explaining such things as assets, liabilities, equity, income, expenses and so forth.

This was very well received and again created a leveraged income stream. Clients paid a fee that may have equated to half or even a quarter of the hourly rate to engage an accountant one-on-one, but with ten participants the effective rate earned was at least double for the firm and often five times. A win-win; the client benefitted from a lower investment and we benefitted from a higher return per hour.

More recently at Straight Talk Group, I was asked to give a shorter version we called 'Understanding Your Numbers' at one of our coaching club meetings. During the process, I identified a huge opportunity for a client and we earned a $33,000 assignment over eleven months to assist them with their marketing strategies. The client was happy and so were we.

The other benefit we gained from these types of sessions was the curiosity they bred in our clients. Because they now understood the numbers better, they felt comfortable asking questions; and when they asked questions, they were asking for advice, and when they asked for advice we had the opportunity to improve their outcomes and earn some compensation for helping them. Another win-win!

It gets better too, from a professional development perspective. When we first rolled out these sessions at 2IC Management, we also witnessed members of our team growing personally through their involvement in the presentations. Although quite coy initially, many of our team grew in confidence with each session they delivered.

In-House Seminars

Very similar to Group Training Sessions, In-House Seminars provide an opportunity to offer a value add service to your clients and charge a fee to deliver them. There is a strong adage that suggests you should charge for your time in delivering these seminars: 'People do not value what they receive for free.' If someone registers for a seminar and you provide it for free, there is a much higher incidence of no shows. They didn't pay for it so if something comes up it doesn't matter to them if they miss it. Whereas if they pay a fee, even if nominal, they are much more likely to attend.

Saying that, we really didn't want to charge a fee for some of our sessions because we didn't want to put any barriers to clients registering. You see, there is a difference between valuing what you don't pay for and actually convincing someone to invest in the first place.

One strategy we used went like this:

> *We hold these events to provide an extra benefit to you our valued client and provide this to you for FREE with our compliments. As we cater for these functions we incur a small cost per participant and do so with our pleasure. However, we do ask to reserve your place you provide a credit card authority for a catering charge of $15. If you*

> *attend the seminar we will not charge the fee. If,*
> *however, you are unable to attend and someone*
> *else has missed the opportunity reserved by you we*
> *reserve the right to debit your credit card.*

There is also a strong argument that if you price it high enough it must be good so people will not want to miss out. But make sure it is good!

The issue here is not so much to make a profit from holding an event but to invite clients to seek your assistance as a result of the information you provided at the seminar. Just like the 10X model and what we experienced with training sessions, by giving clients more knowledge they then know what to ask for help with.

We held several seminars where our team did the delivery, but there were times when we brought in specialists to deliver. Just because you hold a seminar using an outside specialist does not mean there is not the potential for an assignment for your firm. If we introduced a client to a lawyer, HR consultant, financial planner, insurance consultant, or other service provider we never encouraged the client to engage these specialists without our involvement.

Why?

Because too often I have seen advice or direction from these consultants that counter the strategies or specific peculiarities of your client, and quite often the client doesn't understand their position well enough to know how to explain it appropriately to the outside specialist.

Two reasons come to mind.

Firstly, a particular consultant may recommend a strategy that relies on tax deductibility to make it viable, or they use the highest marginal tax rate to justify the plan. Often clients will be excited by these offerings without considering they have carried forward tax losses or only pay tax at 30%.

In the early years at Sims Richmond I was upset when a client told me he was leaving. I asked him what the other accountant was offering that was better than we did. He replied that he had convinced him that he was a tax specialist in his industry. My reply still rings in my own ears: 'Fred, you have never paid tax while you have been with me!' Obviously, I was up against a pretty sweet talker!

Secondly, financial planners will often base a level of life insurance on the balance of all loans associated with a client so his partner will not be left with the burden of these loans. The client generally thinks this is a good idea, except, in reality, there are many options to either sell off surplus assets to pay off some of the loans or some of the loans are very positively geared investments and would not need paying out. I have helped many clients reduce the level of cover initially quoted by the insurance agents. In the end, the agent agreed (and he got a sale), the client was happy and I was the catalyst for the positive result.

The other factor to consider is that in most of the types of outside consultants there is some nexus to financial statements or financial circumstance that will require your assistance.

The overall aim of these referrals is, again to help the client succeed; for example, better protected or less stressed. The result is you are the hero for sorting out the issues and, even if you did not charge for your involvement, who do you think they will call when their next problem or major decision arises?

~6~

Cashflow

'If I had to run a company on three measures, those measures would be customer satisfaction, employee satisfaction and cashflow.'

Jack Welch
Former CEO General Electric

Controlling Cashflow

Accounting practices are typically poor cashflow businesses. Accountants are usually the last to get paid. Yet, cashflow is something that is totally within the control of the principals of the business.

Compliance Work

Why are we not surprised when we encounter fee resistance for compliance work? The basic fundamentals of compliance work is that clients don't want it: they wouldn't volunteer to do it if they weren't forced by legislative compulsion. Then you send them a bill for doing something they didn't want to do. And then the ATO sends them a bill as well.

How can we ever expect a client to look at this and say nice things about the encounter?

The other growing concern is that cloud technology is only going to make it worse because your fees for doing this type of work is going to be under even more downward pressure. The profession is also heading down the same downward spiral of many industries—discounting! The bigger firms are attacking smaller fee compliance work with the view to building relationships. To do this they are dropping their fees. Other firms are aligning themselves with outsourcing firms, either local or overseas, and are using discounting as a marketing strategy.

The only way you can avoid getting caught up in this cycle and encountering fee resistance is to offer value add services. By providing more value than just a compliance service your fees can never be compared legitimately with those of compliance practitioners. It is also very difficult to compare fees between consulting firms offering value add services because the nuances and peculiarity of what you are involved with in your client's business is very hard for a competitor to know until they do the work. What's more, if you are doing a good job, your client will become so reliant on you the fee is not the critical issue.

Put Your Fees Up 15% Across the Board

When we attended the Accountants' Boot Camp in 1999, we were encouraged by Ric Payne and Paul Dunn to go back to our firm and increase our fees by 15%. They were adamant we were undercharging and, given the relationship accountants had back in 1999 of a trusted advisor, it was unlikely there would be any pushback.

We did it at 2IC Management and had very little if any problems. Obviously, our clients did value the relationship they had with us and this also reinforced our confidence as their trusted advisor. However, I'm not sure the same principles would apply to a pure compliance firm today, but for a firm with strong rapport and client engagement it probably would work. But if you provide a once a year tax factory service I would suggest fees are already a very relevant issue.

Clients Prefer Time Payments

I have successfully implemented time payment arrangements that provide yet another win-win for the clients and the accounting firm.

Ask any client whether they would prefer to get a bill at the end of their work, which is required to be paid within fourteen to thirty days upon receipt of the invoice, or to pay it off in instalments over six to twelve months. The answer will be in instalments 90% of the time. Those that prefer a one-off payment are either those that simply want to drag out payments, and probably those with whom you should not deal with, or are highly liquid and pay within the fourteen days and therefore are not a contributing factor to cashflow issues.

Many practitioners have a fear they will get pushback from clients if they offer this type of payment option. I have implemented this with clients who were traditionally paying us on the old payment system and with new clients that have joined the practice through acquisition or from referral. I can only think of one client that didn't buy-in. This client fell into the second category above; never challenged fees and always paid on time. Nonetheless, in recent years even this client has come on board with regular monthly fees for consulting assignments.

Of course, to offer time payments that will benefit you requires starting the repayment programme before the work is completed. Otherwise all that's achieved is giving your clients six to twelve months to pay off a debt you normally hoped would be paid in thirty days.

This is where fixed price billing provides the opportunity. If you address this at the beginning of the year, then both you and your client know what the fee will be and the payment cycle can start as soon as this is established. The end result is some clients pay the majority of their fee before you have even started their work. What's more, they love the idea because they don't get any payment shocks during the year. Conversely, some clients end up paying you after the work has been completed. The bottom line is everybody gets an even spread of cashflow, which is another win-win.

The other benefit is that any issue of fee resistance can be minimised or possibly eliminated. You have the opportunity to discuss the fee before you commence the work and sort out any issues. Quite often the solution is as simple as removing part of your service offering that the client doesn't value or educating the client to present their records in a different way. Compare this to where a fee charged after the event is outside a client's expectations. Sometimes the accountant will only realise they have a problem when they receive an ethical letter from another accountant telling them the client is leaving.

Of course, when implementing change you need to position the proposal in a way that is attractive to your clients. The benefits to the client are outlined above and these benefits should be highlighted in the proposal.

Two other variations to the client proposal are:

1. Once you have had clients on a fixed price arrangement for a year they become used to paying a monthly amount. The process of establishing exactly what their new fee will be for the following year takes time to analyse the prior year's work performed and the fee charged for every client. At 2IC Management, we designed a letter that went out in late June each

year which highlighted how much our clients enjoyed the benefits of regular consistent commitments rather than experiencing peaks and troughs. We then asked permission to start the year on the same monthly payment until we established their new VPA. Once established, we would make adjustments over the next couple of months up or down for the remainder of their payment schedule.

2. For practices not confident on the fixed pricing policy, one option is to implement a system to get buy-in from clients to pay an instalment that approximated their expected fees. At 2IC Management, by highlighting the cashflow benefits to our clients, we had a very high uptake on this type of offer.

Some clients' fees do not justify a payment plan over six months, so at 2IC Management we introduced other payment options depending on the type of assignment:

Small Compliance Work:

We would offer our services based on 50% of the fixed fee when work was first given to us and the balance in sixty days.*

One-off Assignments

On one-off assignments we would again offer a fixed price

---

* Warning: We originally set this up with the second 50% on completion. However, we discovered that a lot of WIP was tied up with the client simply not providing all the information needed. We therefore changed the proposal to sixty days based on this being the expected time we would take if all information is provided in a timely manner.

fee, but we would stretch the payments over a time period relevant to the assignment. However, we would always charge a percentage upfront. For instance, depending on the type of assignment, this may be 50% upfront with five instalments of 10%, or some other variation. Remember, there are no rules when you price your work on value.[†]

Still Don't Believe Clients Will Prefer Fixed Fees?

Long before I was convinced of the benefits of fixed fees and value pricing, I was approached by a client to implement my first VPA (before we had even heard of the term). It happened in 1990, when I was still at Sims Richmond. I remember the year because I had just purchased a new family home and I was confined to it with my leg in plaster after yet another medical injury. A client for whom I had been doing a lot of value add work visited me at my new home and posed a question, which went along the following lines:

'Geoff, we are really happy with what you are doing for us and we are not unhappy with the fees, but we don't like the shock of some of the bills when you do a lot of work in a particular month. Is there any way you can come up with a regular amount to pay each month so that we know what we will be paying and will smooth out our payments for your services?'

This initially put me through a number of different

[†] Additional Tip: If you are setting your fees based on value, there is scope to offer a discounted fee for 100% payment upfront. A 5-10% discount can be very attractive to clients with strong liquidity, and given you are not chasing hourly rates the money looks pretty good in your bank.

emotions. Firstly, I was very anxious when the client wanted to discuss fees. Then I was quite exhilarated by the acknowledgement for the work I was doing, as the fees were probably as high or higher than any other client I was personally working on. Finally, I was puzzled and anxious as to how I was going to convince Dennis to agree to this new way of billing. Dennis and I agreed that it was best to give the client what they wanted and so I set a fee at $2,000 per month with my heart in my mouth.

The client came back and said they were happy with that but wanted to pay it by way of $500 per week. This was a huge win-win. The client got the certainty, so did we, and we ended up with $26,000 per year rather than $24,000 we quoted. Not only has this client been one of my most loyal and engaged, they have referred many good clients to me over the years and I still work with them today.

From this positive experience, whenever I started regular value add work with clients that were experiencing peaks and troughs in my fees, I would approach them with the same proposal. I never had one client knock me back.

I guess that is why I was so easily convinced to convert my practice into a value pricing model; I had already been taught by my clients they preferred it.

You then Get Certainty—No Debt Collection Department

How much do you spend employing people to chase debtors or how much time do you spend making those hard to make phone calls?

You held your breath when you sent the bill, not knowing what the reaction would be from your client, and now sixty days later you haven't heard and even worse you haven't been paid. If you get your employee to call and they get a response that the client is going to pay it shortly (The old, 'The cheque's in the mail!'), you still don't know whether you have offended the client and you still haven't been paid.

What happens next is two-fold: either the employee starts to get fed up with the nonsense they get when calling debtors and starts to make some aggressive comments or challenges the client's excuses, resulting in an angry client; or you yourself call the client with sweat running down your brow as to what reaction you will get. If it's not to their satisfaction, you either cave in and discount the fee, or you challenge the client's willingness to pay. Again, the end result is either you or the client are annoyed and angry.

Compare that outcome to what happens when you have an agreed fee with an agreed payment plan *plus* a signed authority to debit the client's account for the agreed fee. Much nicer, isn't it? No phone calls, no challenging clients' excuses, and one redundant debtor collection position. Not to mention the issue of fee resistance being dealt with well before you commence any work.

The only possible pushback or conflict that might arise is if you didn't deliver what the client expected, and that issue has nothing to do with invoicing and debtor collection; it's about quality control and managing client expectations.

~7~

Lockup

'The problem is never how to get new, innovative thoughts into your mind, but how to get old ones out.'

Dee Hock
Founder of Visa

Debtors

The Good, the Bad & the Ugly of the Australian Accounting Profession 2014 Report (GBU Report) indicates a big percentage of firms across Australia have debtor days in excess of sixty days, which represents 16.4% of annual turnover.

The report also indicates the net profit achieved after partners' salaries was 2.8% of annual turnover for the lower quartile and 13.7% for the median quartile. This means that firms in these groupings had in excess of their year's profit tied up in debtors (and we haven't looked at WIP yet!).

In an ideal scenario, if every client had a fixed price VPA, with instalments paid during the year you performed the work, in theory your debtor balance would be *zero* at end of financial year. The result is an additional 16.4% of annual turnover sitting in your bank account.

Work in Progress

The GBU Report also quoted the level of WIP as twenty-eight to forty-three days for median and lower quartile firms respectively. This represents between 7.7% and 11.8% of turnover tied up in WIP. If we call this 10% for the sake of evaluation, then there is a fair proportion of accounting firms with over 26% of their annual turnover tied up in lockup.

Given the achieved net profit percentage of between 2.8% and 13.7%, there is a drain on cashflow from partners' salary of between 12% and 23% of turnover.

Let's put that into perspective: lower quartile partners averaged about $750,000 turnover and median quartile $1,000,000. This means there are partners tipping into their business out of their salary or capital as much as $170,000!*

Although technically lockup is a static number and not a defined annual percentage, such as the 26% implied by the above figures, if you are growing your practice, as most aim to, it could potentially mean any growth achieved actually results in less disposable income. Surely that is not what partners set out to achieve when targeting growth. Yet I am sure there have been many shocks across the industry when a firm achieves the growth targets they set themselves only for the partners find their dividends reduced.

Consider also when inviting a new partner into the practice. How will they feel about contributing 23% of their share of turnover towards funding lockup when they only earned between 2.8% and 13.7%?

It might be more attractive to get a job!

The Effect on the Valuation of Your Practice

So, how much is your lockup costing you? Most practices are now sold on a profit multiple or capitalisation rate rather than the old cents in the dollar formulae. Therefore, if a purchaser is looking for a return on their investment they will reduce the value of goodwill based on the lockup they inherit. Consider the calculations below based on the GBU Report for a median accountancy firm.

---

* The GBU Report imputes a partner's salary at $200,000.

Looking at a sample firm with three different levels of lockup: 90 days, 30 days or negative 10 days.

	A 90 Days	B 30 Days	C 10 Days Negative
Net Profit per Partner	$330,000	$330,000	$330,000
Less Nominal Partner Salary	$100,000	$100,000	$100,000
	$230,000	$230,000	$230,000
Value based on 25% Cap Rate	$920,000	$920,000	$920,000
Less average lockup	$246,000	$82,000	($27,000)
Goodwill Value	$674,000	$838,000	$947,000
Increased Value		24.3%	40.5%

The results for the firm in Column A means missing out on extra profit by paying interest on $246,000 lockup or equivalent opportunity costs of between $15,000-25,000 per annum per partner.

Column B has reduced its lockup to thirty days and has saved most of the interest and improved its value by 24.3% or $164,000 per partner.

Column C has $27,000 to invest (or take a good holiday) with no lockup and added 40.5% to the value or $273,000 per partner.

The big question is: why do practitioners continue to run their business in a way where they are going without cashflow and having a major downward effect on the value of their business? Especially when there are strategies that will solve these problems and their clients will embrace them?

Why Would You Buy Fees?

This leads us to the question: 'Why would you ever want to buy fees?'

If you are looking at a buy-out of a retiring principal, then you will inherit an enormous amount of legacy from the days gone by. Fair chance the practice has been in existence for decades and every client has been indoctrinated in the 'way we do it here'. From most of the philosophies I have espoused in this book, this scenario is not going to be very attractive.

There is also almost certainty that the clients of such a practice are used to the 'way things are' as well, especially the lockup dilemma we've been discussing. This means that your investment is not just the contract price on the business sale agreement[†], but also the fact that from Day 1 you will be accumulating WIP and after day thirty, sixty or possibly ninety, this will turn into debtors.

The lockup issues can be addressed, but it will not happen overnight. As I have explained, clients actually prefer to be paying their fees over a period of time than get the shock invoice at the end of the job, invariably followed by the tax invoice.

[†] Plus GST, which causes another cashflow issue, as it is unlikely that a merger purchase will be considered a going concern.

What classification are the clients going to fall in with regard to your A, B and C criteria? There is no way they will be all A-class according to your criteria, so you will either have to change their culture and mindset, or move them on. In either event, you will either move on clients you just paid good money for or some will leave having rejected your attempts to change their mindset. In all, your ROI just went down.

Having fallen for this mistake in the past, I can also point out the other collateral damage you will incur. If the buy-out includes staff coming across with the clients, they also are used to 'the way we did it here'. Now, these new team members are quite likely good people and potentially excellent workers, but they have been upset already by the pressure of change. Will the new boss like them? Will they be good enough in the new firm? Will they fit in? Will they still get a car park, early knock off to pick up the kids, and so forth?

Furthermore, on top of all that stress they then get told we don't invoice clients 'that way here'. We are going to tell Bob, Jim and Pat that we don't look after this type of clients. But they have had good relationships with Bob, Jim and Pat, so that doesn't seem fair to them. Guess what? They don't fit in from Day 1 and I guarantee a big percentage never will. They certainly didn't in my experience. And imagine the feedback they are giving your newly purchased client base!

The stress this whole arrangement puts on your existing team and you can be enormous. Of the fee base I purchased, there were a few clients that appeared to be of the type I wanted to deal with. Several used the forced change of accounting firm as an opportunity to move elsewhere as they had been thinking of it for some time but were too loyal to upset the previous owner. I even had one of the inherited employees resign and work on a casual basis for one of the desired new clients. Even after a number of attempts to impress the client, the employee eventually drove the wedge between us and the client left us.

The problem is trying to impress the many clients who have come to you under instructions from a vendor, but there simply isn't enough time to see all of them in a short space of time. Compare this to having a meeting with one new client at a time who has come to you of their own choice. The client who has approached you is looking to be sold to whereas the others often resent being sold off.

The stress that follows from uncomfortable meeting after meeting with unknown receptions is all part of what you need to prepare yourself for. Then, most importantly, what will be your ROI? I mentioned earlier that the GBU Report suggests partners earn between 2.8-13.7% of annual fees. Discount this for the lost clients, potential employee dismissal costs, lockup inherited and throw in some value for stress and it doesn't look very rosy.

All of this suggests that a strategy to grow your client base via referrals and getting closer to understand your clients' needs will provide a less stressful and financially rewarding outcome.

How does spending money on engaging clients sound?

~8~

Business Model

'Connect the dots between individual roles and the goals of the organisation. When people see that connection, they get a lot of energy out of work. They feel the importance, dignity, and meaning in their job.'

Ken Blanchard and Scott Blanchard

Vision and Mission

One of the first things I did when I ventured back to the office after the Accountants' Boot Camp run by RAS was to work with my team on a vision for the business. The second thing I did was raise fees by 15% based on the recommendations of Paul Dunn and Ric Payne.[*]

Unless you know where you want to get to then you can't plan how to get there. But it's even more important that you get buy-in from your team so everybody is on the same bus. That's why it's so important to involve your team in shaping the vision and future of any business.

It's not so much as having the business heading in a direction chosen by your team, but to actively consult with them regarding the direction you want to head in and to glean suggestions from them on some of the details of how to achieve this. Sometimes it means sowing seeds of ideas that your team will latch onto and offer suggestions. Team members are much more likely to follow strategies they feel they have devised than being told by a domineering captain which way to go. I've found that the best outcomes usually stem from their contributions and ideas that enhance your strategies in ways you may not have even considered.

It also means your team can see what opportunities are going to develop for them. If they are made of the right calibre, this will encourage them to perform at higher levels to get to where they want in the business. Conversely, if they are not up to the challenge, they will effectively help manage themselves out of the business because they will realise they haven't got what it takes.

---

[*] See Chapter 6, *Put Your Fees Up 15% Across the Board.*

The alternative to not working with team members on devising the vision for your business is to leave them in the dark. This just alienates them, however. Team members start double guessing where the firm is going and quite often will get it wrong. More so, key employees may start to seek employment elsewhere based on misconceived perceptions of what their future may be.

Once you have identified your vision, it is also a good policy to develop a mission statement with your team as well. This is aimed at setting the standard your clients will come to expect and given your team have assisted in documenting it they will be more inclined to walk the talk.

Structure

Let's spend a moment to talk about the structure of your business.

Team Breakdown

One of the most common forms of inefficiencies in accounting practices is that highly qualified team members carry out tasks that could be performed by someone much less experienced (and therefore less expensive).

To develop an efficient team structure, we at 2IC Management had a motto of encouraging people to push work down the line and for team members to attempt to perform work that may in theory be above their level of experience (obviously with the necessary quality controls and review mechanisms).

The result was that the higher skilled team members were available for the more complex tasks and the less experienced team members grew in abilities faster.

To implement this type of structure I recommend considering Client Service Assistants (CSA). A CSA becomes the wingman of one or more senior accountants as an interface with clients. This person can chase clients up for missing information, do routine checks on the ATO Portal, ASIC and so forth, and also have the personal touch, like a personal assistant, when the accountant is unavailable. They should also be trained in the skill of problem solving for the client.

Often principals or senior management return calls to a client who has a query that anyone in the office could have answered. At 2IC Management, whenever a phone message was taken the team member would pose the following: 'So that Geoff can be prepared for your issue when he calls you back, can I tell him briefly what the call is about?' Quite often the caller will say, 'I just need to know my tax file number,' or something as simple as this. The team member was then able to say, 'I can help you with that,' and solve their problem.

I also made a point of educating my clients that other team members could deal with the minor issues. When I had a call along these lines I would say: 'OK, that is an area where Jennie can help you much faster than me, if you would like to hold the line I'll get her to help. Before I go is there anything else you need help with at the moment?'

Support Team

When computing systems were first introduced, we had specialist keyboard entry employees who would process all the bank statements, journals and so forth. This enabled the accountants to better utilise some of their precious time because of the delegation of data processing.

With the advent of personal computers, and every accountant having a computer on their desk (and now as many screens as you can fit), much of this delegation has gone the other way. Software these days make it easier for accountants to do a lot of the data entry as they go, but there is still a lot of work being performed 'up the line' that should be 'down the line'.

Quite often this is as a result of poor training of the less experienced team members. In many industries, a junior comes to the senior for an answer to a problem and the senior gives them the answer on a plate. Quite often the same query will raise its head down the track but the junior has not learned from the previous instance and requests the same assistance. Whereas, if the senior had posed the question, 'What do you think the solution is?' the junior would have been encouraged to think for themselves and in all likelihood learned a good deal of problem solving.

The same applies in an accounting practice, but too often principals or senior accountants find errors or are handed half-finished jobs and choose the easier option of: 'It will be quicker if I finish it myself.' The junior is more than happy to continue to offload the responsibility, thinking they can't get it wrong if they don't make a decision!

When I was a junior I recall being very annoyed at partners telling me what I had done wrong and giving me back the file to fix. I concluded that they spent more time walking down the corridor, giving me the instructions, me walking back up the corridor, them reviewing it again, than if they fixed it themselves. It was only some years later after I had been employing people for a while that I realised why.

I know plenty of principals do ensure the delegated work is completed by the responsible person, however there are plenty that still do the work. More so, there are even more managers who fail to ensure that the responsible person does what they are employed to do or to train them to do it properly.

Just as we need to train junior accountants to do the tasks allocated to them and to continuously upskill them, we can utilise the strengths of some of the support team to take on administrative roles so often performed by accountants.

One of the principles I would use and encourage clients to use was as follows: if a team member came to me with a problem I would ask, 'What do you think?' If it was a complex issue, I would try and work through it with them and turn it into a learning experience for them. If it was something within their skillsets or something they could stretch themselves to solve, I would ask them to go away and come back with either a number of suggested solutions or at least a list of the issues we needed to address to solve the problem.

This is no different to when a professional, whether an accountant or lawyer, tells a client their strategy won't work for some statutory or legal impasse (for example, tax, commercial law, industrial law and so forth). I've seen this type of advice many times and been frustrated. Our attitude was always to say there is this problem, it won't work how you have it planned but let's look at what we can do to make it work. We would also challenge negative legal advice we received and suggested, 'OK, the law says we can't do that, how can we make it work within the law?'

By implementing systems to make life easier for principals and accountants, the support team can manage a great deal of responsibility. They also learn a lot more and the good ones advance into areas that would normally be a role of an accountant.

~9~

Systems

'I value self-discipline, but creating systems that make it next to impossible to misbehave is more reliable than self-control.'

Tim Ferriss

Systems that Work

Having delegated the responsibility to my team from a very early stage, I had the responsibility to approve systems in the practice and the fulfilment of watching them work. I was fortunate to have young accountants that worked with my key support team to design systems to make work a lot easier. As the accountants grew in their career path, they were able to help fine tune the systems because they understood how they were created and the purpose for which they were designed.

We will now discuss some of the systems that we implemented to improve the efficiency and service of our practice.

Workflow

Communicating with Clients

At 2IC Management, we advised all clients when we had scheduled their compliance work for the coming year and invited them to contact us if that wasn't appropriate. This certainly was a good tool for managing clients' expectations.

Monitoring

With the assistance of the compliance software, we had one of our support team regularly updating our status on where jobs were at, were they on time with promised completion dates, what was holding them up, and so forth. From here we were able to communicate with clients that their job was being held up because they or some other body like a bank or an investment fund had not provided us with the necessary information. Again, this was an excellent way to manage client expectations.

It can certainly be an awkward situation if a client's work has been sitting in the office for six months only to find they haven't provided the extra information you had requested half a year ago. You can't really tell the client it's their fault when you hadn't asked for the missing information a second time.

Billing

Clear Explanation

Most billing software has the ability to set up standard paragraphs such as "Preparation and typing of Tax Returns" but quite often these lose the personal touch because they don't specifically describe the work for each client. At 2IC Management, we made a point of editing the wording for a lot of clients *once* and then used that template for further years.

It is also important to clearly explain other work performed that isn't part of the standard annual work. This is less of an issue once a firm adopts Value Pricing Fees because there is always a well-defined scope of work before work commences. However, when using a time billing system, it makes sense to ensure you outline exactly what you have done, especially if you expect to get paid for it.

Save on Principals' Time

Principals spend a considerable amount of time wading

through time sheets to earmark the extra work outside the scope of compliance work. Analysing months of time sheet entries is another area that does not require the work of a senior partner, but that is normally what happens in an accounting firm. By empowering a support team member to dissect the time sheets into various projects and assignments, we were able to delegate many hours to less senior employees. Of course, once you have trashed the time sheets, you have saved everybody's time.

Benefits of VPAs

A great deal of work on billing is diminished with fixed price VPAs. There is no need to isolate time and dollars on each project if you have agreed on the fee before you start. The only time you need to carry out this analysis is if there appears to be a major blowout on time or scope.

Scope Creep

Just a Quick One:

One problem we all encounter is the call from the client for 'Just a quick one' that turns into a ten-hour job. If you haven't asked for a budget beforehand and fixed a VPA, then you are at the coalface of potential conflict. The client thought it was a quick one, you in all good faith chased the problem up the proverbial drainpipe and now suddenly you are looking to recover several thousand dollars.

It's even worse when the client calls you back or you follow him back for a bit more information and he says, 'Oh, sorry, I forgot you were looking into that, I've sorted it out thanks.'

The only solution to this is for you and your team to have

confidence to raise the issue of fees before you spend more time than you and the client envisaged.*

Sundry Work Clause:

We did have a bit of a 'catch all' clause on our VPAs that said words to the effect that everybody agreed we were entitled to raise an invoice for up to $250 plus GST for any minor assignment where a VPA had not been agreed. Other than that, we had a guarantee that we would not raise an invoice for anything that we had not first discussed and agreed on a VPA before we started work.

What's Your Budget?:

This is a very important factor once you commit to VPAs. You and your team need to be armed and ready to ask the following question: 'That sounds like it might be outside the scope of our agreed VPA, how important is it to you? Do you have a budget I can work to so I can help?'

This puts the client in a very clear position; he is going to pay for the extra help if he wants it. We actually had our team stick a post-it note on their phone with 'What's Your Budget?' written on it.

KPIs

At 2IC Management, we measured KPIs internally among the team and had a master spreadsheet where every team member, including me, would complete a worksheet on an

---

* See *What's Your Budget?* below.

Excel file which was accumulated and displayed at our team meetings. Some of the items we logged were:

1. Fee complaints: These basically disappeared once we converted totally to VPAs.

2. Other complaints: If a client wasn't happy we wanted to know. As I have mentioned before, a complaint is an opportunity to create an advocate.

3. Failures: People were encouraged to highlight mistakes so the team could help coach or counsel each other in order for all of us to learn from our mistakes. We constantly highlighted the fact that mistakes were opportunities in disguise. First time mistakes were never anything to do with the person and all about the process; it happens, but not more than once.

4. Wins: We always liked to celebrate our wins. Big wins brought out the champagne or early knock off for Friday drinks.

5. Impromptu Visits / Phone calls: A way of engaging clients is to call in and see them or phone them without an agenda or invite.[†]

6. Satisfaction Feedback: Each team member would rate how they thought clients felt about what we were doing and how they felt about what we were doing. We rated it between minus five for bad to plus five for amazing. Not often will a team member offer their negative feelings even if they are invited to, however by asking them to rate their feelings it stands out if some-

---

[†] Refer to my comments on WOW factor.

one is not happy. From there you can decide if it's just because their footy team isn't going well or if there is an issue that they need to be heard on.[‡]

7. New Clients / Entities: It is good for the team morale to hear when we won a new client and especially to acknowledge if a team member won them. By highlighting the process we went through, what worked and why we were successful, the whole team felt part of the win.

8. Clients Lost: On the reverse side, the team needs to know if there has been a huge mistake that lost a client. Was it our fault, circumstances outside our control, and what can we learn from it?

9. Seminars attended: Smaller firms are often up against it compared to mid-tier and Big 4 firms with regard to providing adequate training. Quite often this can be a throwaway line or complaint used by employees when someone is disgruntled for other reasons. The truth is, they often like to be hand fed training but aren't committed to do the extra yards themselves. By logging attendances, we encouraged people to go to courses. It is then left back in their court whether they had the expected training. I have found the importance of technical training diminishes when the onus is on the employee to decide to attend.

A few extra words on seminars. Rather than having the whole professional team attend a training seminar

---

[‡] Refer to my comments on Team KPIs.

(sometimes with little value in hindsight), we tended to allocate team members to attend. They would then present a summary of key learnings at our next team technical training session, directing the rest of the team where to go for full details.

I must say, though, most of the seminars I attended over the years were more of a comfort factor than learning experience. That is, they reassured me that I actually knew enough about the particular topics being presented and what I was doing in the business. In fact, I firmly believe I learned more over dinner or at the bar at conferences than attending the technical sessions. Talking to peers about what they were doing, what frustrated them, how they were dealing with issues, and so forth was often more insightful for me.

Sure, I did learn a lot at some sessions, particularly with the ever-changing legislation accountants have to deal with, but for me that's the starting point. The technical stuff is necessary to have a handle on, but that's what you engage specialists for. Knowing enough to realise something was amiss and raising the alarm meant I could have one of our team do the research or engage a specialist lawyer or accountant. Whereas, learning what is happening down in the trenches only comes from chatting with other practitioners.

Renewing VPAs

Once you have set up VPAs for your whole client base (and this doesn't have to be created in one year, it can be grouped into various categories of clients and each year another group brought on board until everyone is converted), the job of reviewing and renewing them can become systemised.

At 2IC Management, we were able to set up a spreadsheet exported from our time-cost system where each fee was listed and various other comparisons logged, such as WIP, write-offs, and write-ups. This allowed the principal to go through the list and assign the adjustment for the forthcoming year. The support team then have template letters depending on the type of adjustment.

As this process can sometimes drag out, we devised a system where we simply sent a letter asking permission to continue debiting their account for the same amount as last year until we provided the revised VPA. We learned early that if we waited to start debiting a monthly fee until the VPA was finalised, we accumulated client resentment. They were not happy with the need to catch-up two, three, four or even five months that had passed until the VPA was agreed. This reinforced our belief that clients preferred the fees be spread over a full year rather than lumpy bills to pay at the end of the assignment, or in this case over several months just to catch up.

Newsletters

As accountants, we are constantly the butt of 'boring' jokes, and when I see the newsletters that are sent out it's no wonder why!

Many years ago, we subscribed to the white-labelled newsletters that half the profession did, simply so we could say to our clients we had a newsletter that we would pass onto them. Because these were written by accountants they were as boring as watching paint dry. The feedback we got was that hardly any of our clients read them. After all, how many motor mechanics, retailers or builders are interested in the tax case on Part IVA or other technical accounting jargon?

After cancelling our newsletters for a number of years, we accessed a white-labelled newsletter with interesting business tips from Principa as a basis for our own newsletters. We added our own particular slant, as we did not want to fall into the trap of being too generic or overloading our clients with information. We decided to provide our own paragraph or two and only use part of the Principa newsletter.

However, there were a lot of teething problems. When some partners or senior employees were rostered to write a piece for the newsletter, it invariably got delayed and the newsletter never went out on time. Eventually, it brought down the whole process. We eventually decided we weren't going to add anything technical to the Principa Newsletter, but instead add more human interest stories. So we had the support team write the copy. As a team, we would decide on interesting topics, whether it was about any clients head-lining the news or personal news about one of the team.

And it worked! The newsletter got processed and sent out on time (well, nearly on time, but it certainly became a lot more regular). Again, this is an important reminder that we were dealing with people. People like to look at and read about people they know. As our clients knew a big percentage of our team, they were interested in reading about them.

~10~

Value Add Services

'The way to a customer's heart is much more than a loyalty program. Customer evangelists is about creating experiences worth talking about.'

Valeria Maltoni

Business Consulting

This book is not going to train anyone on business consulting techniques. The point I would like to make is that if you do not have business consulting as a significant fee contributor in your accounting practice you are going to have to design a very slick organisation to make a dollar. The current traditional accounting and tax practice cannot survive.

Once you start offering ongoing business consulting it has its own life and grows as a natural force. Basically, it works this way: initially, the client asks a question that leads to more work or another assignment. This then grows until eventually they won't make a material decision without your input. From there they start to tell their colleagues how they had some success with a particular issue and they give you a pat on the back. Then new clients start knocking on your door.

In 1998 I was having lunch with very dear clients who operated an advertising agency. Back in the 80s the advertising industry did half their business in pubs and restaurants and Ken and David were convinced they had developed their best campaigns over a nice bottle or two of red wine.

Ken and David had not grown out of the 80s and still lived this ethos into the 90s. Occasionally I joined them. On one occasion, they introduced me to a friend and colleague, Bernie. The following week David called and suggested I give Bernie a call as he would like to talk to me about changing accountants. David's comment was that Bernie had called him and said, 'That accountant of yours seemed like an OK bloke, is he any good?'

I ended up meeting with Bernie and had a very good relationship with him for a number of years. I always remembered that the enquiry was more about personality than any professional impression I made; we certainly weren't discussing tax strategies at the lunch. Unfortunately, the profession does not have a steady stream of training for accountants in this area. Most practices are driven by compliance and deadlines, so the team members do not get exposed to learning how to give advice. Eventually, they get promoted because they have been around long enough or because partners are looking for succession plans. These new senior accountants then find themselves needing to give advice because they are being asked for it, not because they are proactive. In fact, most of the time they would look to duck for cover and send clients off to specialists or lawyers rather than run the risk of the client finding out their shortcomings.

I have had discussions with a number of principals who have said things along the line of, 'We won't go near that stuff, we would get an expert to advise our client.'

I have even sat in a practice meeting where a partner explained how his client believed his business partner was stealing from the business. The accounting partner then went on to ask did anyone know specialists on hotels who we could engage to help. I asked the question, 'Don't we know how to review records and identify these things? Why does it have to be a hotel specialist?' The point is, the issue was outside the norm and even partners shy away from stepping outside their comfort zone.

Another example of a firm shirking their responsibility in this area happened nearly a decade earlier in 1989. I had a new client referred to Sims Richmond who ran a service station in the northern suburbs of Adelaide. John was referred by a long-term client who I had built a strong relationship with and suggested, 'If anyone can help you, Geoff can.'

John, though, was a nervous wreck. He had invested his whole life's savings in his business and was picturing it all going down the toilet. I'll never forget my first impression of him. John was a motor mechanic by trade, a six-foot-four man-mountain who walked into my office a dishevelled mess. He all but teared up when he told me the advice from his accountant: 'You can't make any money in this business. I suggest you sell for whatever you can get.'

Having had experience in this industry while at TG Young & Rendell, I was quite surprised that a site of this type in this location couldn't make money. Something had to be wrong. The oil company involved, like most of them, was very ruthless but their model was to ensure operators made enough to keep them viable, but only enough so that the oil company had maximum returns.

On the surface his gross profit margins looked acceptable, but when we looked closer these margins had been bolstered because he didn't actually buy and sell fuel. He operated a site where he only sold the fuel on behalf of the oil company and was paid a monthly commission for doing so. This commission was included in sales, and since there was no cost of goods sold the resultant gross profit was inflated to look acceptable.

I looked at his numbers and asked him to get me some extra information. Soon we discovered that he was selling stock at way below his expected margins. Together we eventually broke it down to his milk sales, of all things. It turned out he was selling milk for less than he was getting charged by the milk company, Farmers Union. We discovered that the night manager had teamed up with the milk deliverer to doctor the invoices and split the profits. This milk scam was costing John thousands of dollars a week, and that was back in the 1980s.

The good news is that he sorted out the thieves, ran the business at a healthy profit for a number of years, eventually sold it for a nice sum and bought into the hotel and liquor industry. He did very well thereafter.

I will always remember this assignment, not because I got the numbers right but because I was able to help a person who had been told they were financially ruined, someone who got to fight another day and in fact become very successful financially.

This is an example of an opportunity that can present itself for anyone accustomed to working closely with their clients' numbers. But many accountants seem unsure where to start with the countless opportunities that present to them from their current clients. Yet, it's actually quite easy to start the ball rolling on business consulting. I was able to consistently build clients fees many times over what they paid their previous accountant and have them as my best referrers because of one simple reason: they actually got a return on the fees they invested in their accountant.

By simply having a conversation with a business client, you can start to identify their concerns, needs and shortcomings that you may be able to offer some assistance. If you also follow the Sims Richmond motto of no set of financial statements leaving the premises without some comment or advice, this also develops enquiries from clients.

Here are some of the ways we generated further business consulting income from our clients.

Efficiency Analysis Report

Once you have a set of financial statements you can ask a client how they price their products and services. From here, it is very easy to highlight the shortfall on their results compared to their costing formula.

A client becomes very interested when you point out that if they actually achieved results in line with their quoting formula they should have earned an extra $100,000.*

Breakeven Analysis Report

Many businesses do not fully grasp the concept of contributions versus sales. Therefore, highlighting to your clients what is needed to be sold to breakeven or make a desired level of profit perks their interest as much as an Efficiency Analysis Report

Goal Setting

If you aim at nothing you will hit it with a great degree of regularity.

Helping clients set goals is one of the most important steps in any business. It's their goals, all you need to do is help them document them and at the same time challenge them to make sure they are SMART.† Once you have set them, you help them monitor them.

Monitoring—The Hawthorne Effect

At 2IC Management, we always promoted the concept *if you*

---

* See below, *Initial Interview*.
† Specific. Measurable. Achievable. Results focused. Time related.

can measure it you can manage it. We had countless examples of how monitoring client results improved their business KPIs. Later, I discovered there was an accepted psychological or even economic term for this: The Hawthorne Effect.

The Hawthorne Effect (also known as the observer effect) is a type of reactivity in which individuals modify or improve an aspect of their behaviour in response to their awareness of being observed. From our perspective, business owners and employees will improve their performance just because it is being monitored.

Initial Interviews

I mentioned in Mistake No 5 that when I was younger, and before I understood the difference between time and value, I was focused on what fee I could generate from a new client. Eventually, I realised the value the client attributed to our relationship was not based on how much work I did for them but what value I produced. From there I changed my way of thinking. At the initial interview with a new client, I still looked at the expense item 'accounting fees' on their profit and loss statement, but this was more to understand the budget they may be considering.

I found it easy to impress or at least stimulate business owners in situations where they were asked to quote for the sales they achieved. This was especially with a combination of labour and materials or other resources that were a cost of goods sold.

Time and again the conversation would go like this:

> Geoff: *Tell me how you quote?*
> Client: *We charge our time at $85 per hour.*
> Geoff: *And what about materials?*
> Client: *Yes, we charge them at cost plus 50%.*

Geoff: *What about overheads, do you charge anything for them?*

Client: *Yes, we add the wages charge and the marked-up materials together and add 19% for overheads.*

Geoff: *Why 19%?*

Client: *We've always done that. I can't remember where we got that from.*

Geoff: *OK, is that your final price then?*

Client: *No, then we mark all that up by 20% to allow for stuff ups[‡].*

Geoff: *So, that's the final price?*

Client: *Pretty much, but we then look at the job and decide whether it seems too low and might add anything from a few dollars to round it up or a few grand if it's a complicated job.*

Geoff: *So, you really used all your formulas to justify an estimate and then charge what you think it's worth. So, in reality, market pressures dictate your price.*

Client: *I guess so.*

Geoff: *What's your success rate on winning quotes?*

Client: *About 50%.*

Geoff: *Do you have records to prove this?*

Client: *No*

Geoff: *Do you know why you only win 50%?*

Client: *Probably too dear as we don't try and be the cheapest.*

I then quickly look at the client's profit and loss statement and was able to work out how many hours were available

---

[‡] This term had many variations, many of which should not be repeated in this book.

from his wages, multiply this by $85 and go through all the other formulae using the actual costs on the profit and loss.

I then ask: *Are your production team busy?*

> Client: *Yeah, flat out.*
>
> Geoff: *Well, according to my calculations there should be an additional $100,000. If your men are busy, and every quote is carried out on every job how you have just explained to me, then your sales should have been at least $100,000 higher.*
>
> Client: *I don't understand.*
>
> Geoff: *I have simply used your quoting formula and treated all the known components you have spent on jobs for the year and multiplied it out. This means you are either under quoting based on your estimate of time or materials, or your team are slacking off, or someone is ripping you off.*
>
> Client: *No-one would be ripping me off. I trust everybody who works for me.*
>
> Geoff: *I can point to a number of businesses where the owner said just that only to find out different later. But let's assume no-one is ripping you off, would you like to increase your bottom line by $100,000? Or let's just say we can identify an additional $50,000 in efficiency, how would you feel about that?*
>
> Client: *Great!*

The conversation would continue and invariably we win the client over as no-one had ever examined their business like that. What's more, they were always keen to find out how they could improve their business efficiency, which we helped them do.

Consider the increased ROI this client achieves on their

fee investment compared to what they paid their previous accountant.

Unlimited Phone Calls

Once you have engaged clients in value add consulting services, the dollar cost is not the issue but the relationship and their perception of what you bring to their business. One of the first steps compliance firms can do is offer their services to include unlimited phone calls on day-to-day issues at no charge. Immediately you are bundling your package to be different from a pure compliance accountant. Of course, some clients will, deliberately or not, abuse this system so it needs to be clearly defined. But if you keep in mind what I've said earlier on scope creep, you will be fine. Once you start bundling other services you can bring value to the fore versus cost.

The other important fact to consider in offering unlimited phone calls is the extra revenue it will create. I guarantee if you can encourage your clients to call you with issues, between you and the client you will identify an assignment that they are happy to invest in. So, if you compare how much many firms spend on marketing or even buying fees, the offer of unlimited phone calls is much more cost effective. In fact, I maintain it is more of a profitable investment than a cost.

Board of Management Position

Although we never defined it under these terms, I often held an equivalent position with clients in their business as they involved me in so much of their business decision making. Our fees were built in to the overall retainer and it was based on value not time.

The biggest achievement here was the close personal relationships that followed. Many clients became and are still good friends. Gerry and I have attended many clients' birthday parties, weddings, children's weddings, and other private social events.

One of my favourite clients, who certainly reaped the rewards of More Time, More Money and More Fun, was a young entrepreneur named Margie. She developed a street magazine from her lounge room floor to initially selling part of the business to an international media magnate and eventually the remainder for a significant sum. During the years I worked with Margie, I saw her and helped her grow from a couple of staff operating out of a toilet cubicle (her description, not mine) to occupying a two-story office building with a team of approximately twenty. I sat in on her team reviews, helped with presentations to team meetings, worked with her in developing new magazines, and had heaps of fun at a number of social functions and long lunches. We also held her hand through the whole merger and eventual sale.

A real opening these days is for accountants to position themselves as Chief Financial Officers (CFOs) for their clients. Many small enterprises cannot afford a full-time person with your level of qualifications, but they can do with your expertise on an as needs or part-time basis.

One of the first positioning statements I used when I first launched 2IC Management in 1994 was, 'Could one and a half heads be better than two?' Back then Kerry Packer would have been considered one of the most successful businessmen in Australia. I proposed that every business would like to have someone like Kerry on their Board of Management, but they wouldn't be able to afford him. So, rather than have Kerry on your team, why not have 2IC Management on a part-time basis?

Marketing Consulting

Since we transcended from an accounting firm to our offerings under Straight Talk Group, we have developed a marketing consulting service.

As an accounting firm, we never provided specific help in this area. The closest we came was running a number of seminars we acquired from RAS & Principa on customer service. However, if I was running an accounting practice today I would be definitely be offering this service. Sure, accountants are not marketers and you probably haven't got the time on your hand that we had to develop the necessary skills, but you can outsource them.

We started running business improvement seminars as a lead generator for consulting and coaching assignments. As was common practice, we provided feedback forms and invited attendees to suggest other seminars they would like to attend. We soon became aware that marketing solutions was the hottest topic in demand by a street. 'Help me get more clients!' was probably the most common need they wanted most assistance with in their business. That's not too dissimilar to what accounting firms want—more clients!

However, the No.1 rule for all businesses is to market to your existing client and customer base. We teach small business operators to first concentrate on their current client base as it is much easier to sell a product or service to a current customer than to find a new one and convince them to do business with you. Accountants could not only learn to teach their clients this simple philosophy but could learn the lesson themselves.

Closing Comments

If you've made it all the way through this book I thank you for your persistence. I hope it has been helpful and would like to think that you may use it as an ongoing guide that you may even go back to and reflect upon.

I don't for one minute believe I would have blown you away with too much that anyone would conclude isn't just common sense. What I would challenge you and other accountants with is to be honest with yourself. I know, I've been there!

I'm also not on my high horse saying I did all the good things in this book all the time. Of course I didn't. What I did do is develop a team and systems to slowly get a pretty good success rate on a lot of the philosophies and strategies I have highlighted.

I would be very keen to get feedback from anyone who has taken the time to read my suggestions and my contact details can be found at www.geoffrichmond.com

If you would like assistance in implementing any of my suggestions our team at Straight Talk Group would really love to help.

WOW Bombs from Geoff

1. It's ALL ABOUT PEOPLE (see page iii).
2. Don't just develop your employees, develop a Team (see page 39).
3. Accept that 80% correct can be good enough (see page 74).
4. It is your role to delegate. Identify tasks that can be delegated (see page 74).
5. To ensure clients receive the best outcomes and that you have the best resources to deliver them, not only do you need to train your team, you also need to train your clients (see page 76).
6. A simple but effective way to Wow your clients: Incorporate menus into your reception (see page 89).
7. It's not about you! Build engagement between the client and the firm, not the client and the principal (see page 92).
8. Motivate your team without spending on incentives. You cannot expect your team to perform to your expectations if you do not set clear guidelines on what you want (see page 100).
9. Incentives can work, but offer incentives to promote team performance over individual performance (see page 100).
10. KPIs not only measure performance but help with the Hawthorne Effect. Keep a record of impromptu phone calls to keep it front of mind of your team (see page 113).

11. Professionals prefer not to be salespeople. The fact is, we are acting as salespeople day in day out whether we realise it or not (see page 116).

12. If you want assignments to run smoothly, get your clients to sign a Mutual Commitment Statement (see page 124).

13. You know you will pay for it if it goes wrong, so differentiate yourself and offer guarantees for the service you provide (see page 129).

14. People value what you do for them, not necessarily by the quality of the professional services you provide (see page 140).

15. Build client engagement to differentiate yourself from your competitors (see page 150).

16. Break the seal on business consulting and it has its own life and grows as a natural force (see page 209).

17. Stop spending money on marketing and advertising and start talking to your clients. The No.1 rule for all businesses is to first market to your existing client and customer base (see page 219).

Bibliography

Books that have either been referred to in this book or have had a big bearing on my philosophies:

Baker, Ronald J. *Implementing Value Pricing: A Radical Business Model for Professional Firms*. Hoboken, NJ: John Wiley & Sons, Inc., 2011.

Covey, Franklin. *The 7 Habits of Highly Effective People.* Version 2.0 Singapore: Franklin Covey Co.

Lencioni, Patrick. *Overcoming The Five Dysfunctions of a Team. A Field Guide* San Francisco, CA: Jossey-Bass, A Wiley Imprint,2005.

Lewis C. Patrick. *Building a Shared Vision. A Leader's Guide to Aligning the Organisation*. Portland Oregon: Productivity Press,1997.

Lund, Dr Paddi. *Building the Happiness-Centred Business*. 2nd ed. Capalaba, QLD: Solutions Press, 1997.

Lund, Dr Paddi. *The Absolutely Critical Non-Essentials*. Capalaba, QLD: Solutions Press, 1996-2006.

Lund, Dr Paddi. *Mobilising Your Customer Sales Force*. Capalaba, QLD: Solutions Press 1998-2007.

Maxwell, John C. *The 21 Irrefutable Laws of Leadership*. 10th ed. Nashville, Tennessee: Thomas Nelson, Inc. 2007.

Maxwell, John C. *Everyone Communicates Few Connect*. Nashville, Tennessee: Thomas Nelson, Inc. 2010.

Weiss, Alan. *Value-Based Fees: How to Charge—and Get— What You're Worth. A Guide for Serious Consultants*. 2nd ed.cisco, CA: Pfeiffer, A Wiley Imprint 2008.

~Appendices~

Appendix A—Client Survey
Appendix R—Reception Menu / 2IC
          Performance Standards
Appendix C—Coaching Principles in Action
Appendix L—Letter to Your Partner
Appendix K—KPI Spreadsheet
Appendix M—Mutual Commitment
          Statement
Appendix B—7 Biggest Mistakes Business
          Owners Make with their
          Accountant
Appendix F—Happy 29th February Card
Appendix S—Standards Not Met Offer

Appendix A

2IC Performance Standards

Listed below are our documented performance standards. Please let us know how we are going and provide as much detail as you wish with your concerns.

▶ We will always go out of our way to help you when you need our assistance.

Achieved Standard   Failed Standard   Not applicable
⬜   ⬜   ⬜

▶ You will receive your completed tax returns and/or financials within 8 weeks of us receiving your records provided all information received.

Achieved Standard   Failed Standard   Not applicable
⬜   ⬜   ⬜

▶ We will answer the phone within 3 rings.

Achieved Standard   Failed Standard   Not applicable
⬜   ⬜   ⬜

▶ If the person you are calling is unavailable, we will offer the assistance of another team member or ourselves.

Achieved Standard   Failed Standard   Not applicable
⬜   ⬜   ⬜

▶ Your message will be returned by close of business where possible or by midday following day.

Achieved Standard   Failed Standard   Not applicable

☐   ☐   ☐

▶ You will not be left on hold for longer than 1 minute without us checking you are happy to wait.

Achieved Standard   Failed Standard   Not applicable

☐   ☐   ☐

▶ When you call us we will never screen calls.

Achieved Standard   Failed Standard   Not applicable

☐   ☐   ☐

▶ Comprehensive notes will be kept on all dealings with you so that we can ensure we can help you more efficiently in future dealings.

Achieved Standard   Failed Standard   Not applicable

☐   ☐   ☐

▶ We will offer you a drink and refreshments when you come to see us at our office.

Achieved Standard   Failed Standard   Not applicable

☐   ☐   ☐

▶ When we do work for you we will give you a completion date based on the information we have at that stage.

Achieved Standard   Failed Standard   Not applicable

☐   ☐   ☐

▶ When you have your tax returns prepared by us we will phone you within 2 weeks of receiving to ensure total satisfaction.

Achieved Standard   Failed Standard   Not applicable

☐   ☐   ☐

▶ We will never say no unless we consider your request unethical or illegal.

Achieved Standard   Failed Standard   Not applicable

☐   ☐   ☐

▶ You can count on us to be on time for appointments.

Achieved Standard   Failed Standard   Not applicable

☐   ☐   ☐

▶ Our clients will always be our preferred supplier of their products and services.

Achieved Standard   Failed Standard   Not applicable

☐   ☐   ☐

Other ways 2IC could have performed better for you:

Other Comments:

Appendix R

To Make Your Life Easier

Welcome Connor,

We want to make your time with us as efficient, convenient and memorable for you as possible. So, if there is anything we can do for you—anything at all—please feel free to ask.

For example, we would be delighted to:

- Answer your mobile phone, so that you don't miss any urgent messages
- Charge your mobile phone (we have Nokia & Eriksson chargers only)
- Pay for your parking
- Book you a taxi
- Any Photocopying / Faxing / Emailing
- Lend you an umbrella if it's raining when you leave
- Telephone wherever you are going next to tell them when to expect you
- Provide an office to prepare yourself for your next meeting or make any phone calls

Or anything else that makes your life easier. All you have to do is ask and we'll do our very best to help.

Please tick the items you would like below and we will be happy to prepare your choices for you. If you are here for a lunch appointment, please feel free to select a baguette.

COFFEE

☐ Cappuccino
☐ Short Black/White
☐ Long Black/White

SPRING WATER

BISCUITS

☐ Double Choc Chip
☐ Anzac
☐ Apricot & Choc Chip

ALCOHOLIC BEVERAGES

☐ Jim Beam
☐ Gordons Dry Gin
☐ Bacardi
☐ Mildara Brandy
☐ Johnnie Walker Black Label
☐ Ouzo
☐ Stolichnaya Vodka
☐ Beer—Crown, Stella Artois, Coopers
☐ Wine—Red or White

MIXERS

☐ Dry Ginger
☐ Tonic
☐ Soda Water
☐ Coke
☐ Bitter Lemon

TEA

☐ English Breakfast
☐ Earl Grey
☐ Herbal - Green Tea, Peppermint, Raspberry

LUNCH—BAGUETTES

☐ *Caesar Chicken*— chicken, crispy bacon Caesar dressing & cos lettuce

☐ *Smoked Turkey*— smoked turkey, avocado, semi dried tomatoes, pesto & spinach

☐ *Ham*—ham, cheese, tomato, mayonnaise, mustard & lettuce

☐ *Nicoise Tuna*— nicoise tuna, olives, capsicum, semi dried tomatoes, basil, mayonnaise & spinach

☐ *Roast Vegetable*— roast vegetable mix, hommos & roquette

2IC Management Performance Standards

▶ We will always go out of our way to help you when you need our assistance.

▶ You will receive your completed tax returns and/or financials within eight weeks of us receiving your records provided all information received.

▶ We will answer the phone within three rings.

▶ If the person you are calling is unavailable, we will always offer the assistance of another team member or ourselves.

▶ Your message will be returned by close of business where possible or by midday following day.

▶ You will not be left on hold for longer than 1 minute without us checking you are happy to wait.

▶ When you call us we will never screen calls.

▶ Comprehensive notes will be kept on all dealings with you so that we can ensure we can help you more efficiently in future dealings.

▶ We will offer you a drink and refreshments when you come to see us at our office

▶ When we do work for you we will give you a completion date based on the information we have at that stage.

▶ When you have your tax returns prepared by us we will phone you within two weeks of receiving to ensure total satisfaction.

▶ We will never say no unless we consider your request unethical or illegal.

▶ You can count on us to be on time for appointments.

▶ Our clients will always be our preferred supplier of their products and services.

Appendix C

Coaching Principles in Action
by Lisa Ormenyessy

A Business Cannot Outgrow its Leadership

I have seen many times when a business has hit the limit of its leadership. No matter how great the product is, no matter how great they market it, if the business owner doesn't have the skills to leverage the opportunity then it is as good as over, with a good amount of frustration and angst thrown in from the business owner, his staff, suppliers, and the coach.

The business is always a reflection of the business owner.

I remember one business owner coming to me to help get his business ready for sale. He already had a buyer in the wings, however the deal was strategically a year out for the buyer who was wanting to gain geographical area and some of my client's key customers. The owner wanted to use the year to increase the asset value of his business before doing the deal.

The client told me he had some small 'holes' in his business and wanted a 'total overhaul' and 'clean up' (or so he said) and was prepared to pay handsomely for it. When asked how he knew if the business was doing well or not, his response was, 'I can buy a new racehorse with cash.'

It became obvious very quickly that despite his massive turnover, he was a backyard operator who had hit it rich—despite his lack of business knowledge and who thought he could make up the rules as he went along. What he really wanted from the coaching process was someone to not make his business cleaner, but more 'legal' and thought that he could abdicate what was required to do this by throwing money at a coach.

I took him through a very structured process, having him and his team work on different areas of his business each month, documenting it, identifying what changes needed to be made and following up with him and the team. It was very apparent early on that, despite the market being hungry for what he had, because of his lack of leadership and willingness to do things 'right' and to be held accountable for his business, we were fighting a losing cause and no success would come of it.

I illustrated—through the process—that what he thought were 'small pin pricks' were actually gaping holes. His unwillingness to grow, learn and change for the health and success of the business became apparent and he self-selected to opt out of coaching. Although he had a multimillion-dollar business, because of his lack of coach-ability his business fell over within the year.

Which brings to me to my next point for a successful business coaching relationship.

A Business Owner must be Coachable and Willing to Grow.

No matter, how little, or how much knowledge a client has, there is always room for growth.

Recently a young woman with a midwifery business approached me for business coaching. The business was only 6 months old and employed her in a 'job'. With small children, she was running it part-time and had only one referrer who had an on/off personality type which left her at risk of losing her business overnight if he decided to go 'off'.

She had very little business skills or knowledge but a great attitude and willingness to do whatever it took to succeed. She came to business coaching knowing that there were things she didn't know and overwhelmed about her next steps. She fought constantly with fear and what I call the 'Imposter Syndrome'—the fear of getting found out she was just winging it. In fact, she was highly skilled, reputable and on the leading edge of her profession, breaking new ground and creating new markets.

The value coaching she received gave her this backup—knowing she was not alone in creating her business. This has given her the confidence to take big, scary steps and overcome her fear. Help with strategic goal setting and sticking to 90-day goals has removed a lot of overwhelm. Education around what business skills she has needed along with developing the entrepreneurial mindset she needs to succeed has had her develop into a strong leader with resilience.

Through coaching and education, she has changed her method of distribution, decreased the risk to her business by being more strategic in her alliances, referrers and more creative in setting up multiple streams of income into her business.

Three years on she has employed staff, has multiple referrers, an online training program for parents, is sponsored by a major health fund, products that sell while she sleeps, and is just about to sign deals with major grocery retailers for her own branded product aimed at breastfeeding mothers.

As a coach, working with many different businesses and industries I have the advantage of seeing and leveraging ideas, concepts and models from one industry to another. In the aforementioned case, I leveraged a referral strategy that a business in the electrical industry was using and overlayed it on hers.

When a potential client asks me what knowledge I have

of their industry I silently cringe. Not because I may or may not have knowledge of their industry, but because they are missing the whole point of a coaching 'birds eye view' and the concept of leverage.*

The most leveraged coaching model, for both the coach in terms of fees, and for clients in terms of networks, learning and coaching, is the group coaching model, or mastermind groups.

Group Coaching

As well as working closely and having single one-to-one client relationships, I have been running group coaching and mastermind groups for many years now.

By far, the clients who use both of these methods together do the best. Isolation is a killer to creativity, brainstorming and quite simply good mental health. All it takes is one bad day in your business to start the mental slide into negative self-talk. Most business owners I know have experienced this at one time or another.

A successful mastermind removes business owner isolation and acts as a non-executive board for its members, creates a great learning platform, increased accountability and fabulous networking. The knowledge in the room is leveraged as the sum of the members is way greater than the parts.

Just recently one member, a general manager of a multimillion dollar travel group, came to our mastermind exhausted, saying, 'I couldn't afford the time to come today, however I couldn't afford not to come. I need this, I needed to take time out to work on my business and to just 'rest' in the group and feel like I am not alone in this.'

---

* It is also a red flag for a business owner with a 'know it all' syndrome.

Goal Setting and Accountability

We prefer to use a 90-Day model and three months is a decent time to get larger 'tasks' done and breakdown large projects into clearly defined action steps. It also conveniently lines up with a business quarter for reporting. The 90-Day goal setting model is also very strategic because it aligns with the areas for growth in a business that often get over looked. As a busy business owner, it is easy to fall into the trap of 'busyness' vs 'business'. When our to-do list is so long and we fall into overwhelm, it is human nature to do what we are good at and allows us to feel successful and productive at the end of the day. What a business owner is good at, though, may not necessarily be good for the business.

I remember one client who had bought a carpet cleaning business with a silent partner. The silent partner approached me as he couldn't see the profit he had expected flowing from the business. As it turned out, the active partner was sitting at home all day working on spreadsheets (which incidentally he thoroughly enjoyed and could play like a piano). He was working on the business trying to reduce his costs of goods and researching and developing the quality of the products he was using in his business. He knew how to do this—and it came easily to him.

Within himself, he felt he could sleep at night knowing he was being productive and working on his business. The problem with this, though, was the area of growth he was working was the wrong area for the stage the business was at. This was clearly illustrated when we worked on using the structure of our 90-Day plan.

What his business needed to grow was sales. However, driving his number of sales through actively promoting his business and increasing referrals was uncomfortable for him. Using the 90-Day action plan, and its structure on each of the growth points, encouraged him to focus on all areas of his business; not just those he was comfortable with. It opened up a conversation about fear of rejection and an education process around sales and marketing.

A coach will always be on the lookout for those areas of the business that are not being worked on to ensure the business has a strong foundation to build from and there are no gaps that have the potential to topple the business in times of stress.

Time—Money—Leverage

A coach will save you time, money and enable you to leverage your business much quicker than you could on your own. If you are an entrepreneur and momentum is important to you—which it should be—then building a relationship with a coach in a 'no-brainer'.

An experienced and seasoned business coach will have a list of proven referrers for all the resources a business will need, from graphic design, SEO, printers, and best software to trusted professionals like lawyers, accountants and, yes, even a dentist.

Just recently I had two clients embark on a lucrative joint venture. One was in IT services, the other in hosting management. A natural match, but one that would not have happened without an introduction from the coach to each other.

Other examples of joint venture introductions I have made have been between a videographer and business owner using video to promote her profession and her network. The videographer now has a steady stream of clients, and the business owner has increased the trust level with her network and is now getting her videos filmed and produced for very little cost.

Awareness

Awareness is the key to change and consequently growth.

With greater awareness of our own behaviour and how we show up in our business, and greater awareness of our relationships with others and ourselves allows us to see where we may be self-sabotaging our success. A coach will have a wide set of distinctions, and have what is termed in the coaching industry a 'distinctionary'. That will help cut through the clutter and create awareness for their clients so they are then able to make conscious decisions on what is required for growth (for example business vs busyness).

I remember one client who seemed to always have that 'one project' they were continuously working on but couldn't seem to finish. Just one more tweak, just one more idea for it each time we met. It was dragging on and taking way more time and energy than what was initially expected.

As his coach, I was able to share the adage that: *Procrastination is aligned to Perfectionism.* They were able to see their self-sabotaging behaviour, which then led on to a conversation around the concept of 'failing forward'. Within 10 minutes he was able to break through, realign how he was thinking about his project and enabled him to sign off on his MVP (minimal viable product) and complete stage one of his project that day.

Accountability

The accountability structure of a coach provides the impetus to *do* and take action quickly. Many times a client has come to me breathless stating, 'I only just finished that goal we set last month,' slightly embarrassed that they have 'only just' completed it. As a coach, it doesn't matter if you did what you committed to, 5 minutes after our previous session or 5 minutes prior to our current session. What matters most is that you did it!

Clients, I've found, are moved to do a task because it is due. Having a coach measuring your results and holding you accountable to what you said you wanted to do means you are you are going to get better—faster.

Appendix L

Letter to Your Partner

Hi Gerry,

I'm writing this letter to let you know how things are going five years after we set up strategies in June 2009.

How things have changed!

Since I started my four-day week in July 2011 the Team and clients have really embraced my new lease of life and it seems as though it's almost a thrill for them when we engage.

Now that the structure has really settled down I'm looking forward to the 3 day per week schedule which will allow us to have regular long weekends. Can't wait to see the golf handicap improve.

So what's happened over the past 5 years at 2IC Management?

Back in 2008/09 we had fees of approximately $1.7m but that included Jarrad's fees of about $160,000 and a lot of the Stidston Practice which we always intended culling.

So we targeted achieving $1.7m for 2009/10 and achieved that plus some.

Results for the subsequent years were:

2010/11	$2.0m
2011/12	$2.5m
2012/13	$3.2m
2013/14	$3.6m

In addition to this we have added our Coaching Club Business, 10X. This has generated revenues of:

2009/10	$240K
2010/11	$440k
2011/12	$650k
2012/13	$600k
2013/14	$660k

Guess what? The overwhelming debt in excess of $1.0m back in 2009 has now gone... and so have the anxiety attacks!

How has this all been achieved?

THE TEAM has been fantastic! Chris Stewart has grown in leaps and bounds and I am proud to call him a partner. The clients love him and as do the Team and his work ethic is spot on.

Barry Mansfield has now been with me for 27 years and it's great that he has equity in the firm and is also able to wind back his working hours to a four-day week.

The stalwarts are all still with us:

Mark	15 years
Trish	14 years
Jennie	13 years – back part-time after kids.

From 2009 when we had 16 full-time equivalent employees before culling the Stidson and Jarrad clients we have increased this to 19 in 2IC and 2.5 in 10X.

Cashflow has improved by virtue of our billing system finally working how we had been planning even back in 2009. Once we got down to a manageable number of clients it was easy to raise fees up-front before we started and payments were organised by direct debit to the client's bank accounts. All the Senior Accountants have taken ownership of this process which has made life much easier for Ante.

Our team is also very proactive in their attitude to work and clients. This enthusiasm has flowed through the whole team and in fact the marketplace. We actually have experienced accountants approaching us to see if there are any vacancies.

It almost seems like there are no more stress issues to encounter—but we know that is not possible but I can definitely say we have got everything within our control under control.

Love,
Geoff

Appendix K

KPI Spreadsheet

2IC Management Key Performance Indicators				
1/7/20__ - 30/6/20__	Jul	Aug	Sep	Oct
Number of Complaints:				
Number of Fee complaints	0	0	0	**0**
Comments from individual sheets				
Number of Other complaints	0	0	0	**0**
Comments from individual sheets				
Number of 'Failures'	0	0	0	**0**
Comments from individual sheets				
Wins				
Number of 'Wins'	0	0	0	**0**
Comments from individual sheets				
Impromptu Visits				
Number of visits	0	0	0	**0**
Comments from individual sheets				

Nov	Dec	Jan	Feb	Mar	Apr	May	Jun	To Date
0	0	0	0	0	0	0	0	0
0	0	0	0	0	0	0	0	0
0	0	0	0	0	0	0	0	0
0	0	0	0	0	0	0	0	0
0	0	0	0	0	0	0	0	0

KPI Spreadsheet Cont.	Jul	Aug	Sep	Oct
Impromptu Phone Calls / Emails				
Number of phone calls / Emails	0	0	0	**0**
Comments from individual sheets				
Feedback from -5 to +5				
Total:				
Individual perception of what clients think	27	20.5	0	**0**
Individually, how we feel	19.5	17	0	**0**
Comments from individual sheets				

Nov	Dec	Jan	Feb	Mar	Apr	May	Jun	To Date
0	0	0	0	0	0	0	0	
								Average
0	0	0	0	0	0	0	0	3.96
0	0	0	0	0	0	0	0	3.04

Appendix M

The Mutual Commitment Statement

We both agree that the objective of our relationship is to help you achieve your goals and improve your results and it is dependent on both our commitments to making it work and that we will work together to achieve the outcomes and goals we plan for.

Our Commitment to You

1. We will act honestly and with integrity in everything we do for you and with you.
2. We will respect absolutely the confidentiality of our working relationship.
3. We will return your phone calls within 24 hours, even when we are out of the office. When your primary contact is on vacation, we will advise you in advance and arrange for another person in our firm to look after your inquiries.
4. We will meet the deadlines we set with you or we will advise you in advance of our inability to do so for reasons absolutely outside our control.
5. We will give you a firm Value Pricing Agreement for any additional fees for additional projects or assignments, and will discuss any variation that may be necessary before amending any prior fee proposal.

Your Commitment to Us

To achieve your goals and improve your results, a number of commitments need to be made by you:

1. To be open and frank with us at all times and you will advise us of any concerns you have with any aspect of the project we are working on.
2. To willingly implement and test suggestions and insights provided.
3. To implement the projects and actions you commit to at each meeting and make contact if there is anything preventing you from implementing those successfully.
4. To send in regular reports or results on a timely basis as agreed between us.
5. To pay our fee on time as agreed between us.

I understand and accept my commitments:

Signature: _____ Signature: _____

Accepted by_____

Accepted by 2IC Management

The 7 Biggest Mistakes Business Owners Make with their Accountant & How to Turn their Fees into an Investment

How to Find the Accountant You Need for Your Business

Hi there, my name's Geoff Richmond.

Firstly, let me congratulate you on taking a few minutes to read this report. It's not everyone who makes the extra effort to take their business to the next level. And in my thirty-four years as a chartered accountant I've noticed those that do, are those who succeed.

Over my accounting career, and those of the hundreds of accountants I've employed, I've been able to discern 7 Big Mistakes every small business owner must avoid.

As a service to the accounting industry and the small business community that's been so good to me over the years, I'm going to share the 7 Big Mistakes with you. It's my way of giving back, of rewarding the accountants who take value and service seriously, and the businesspeople willing to go the extra distance to engage them.

Accountants—The Great, the Not So Great and the Simply Dangerous

Let me quickly introduce you to the notion of 'normal distribution'. It means in any group there's a small amount of people at either end of any measurement with the great bulk being somewhere in the middle. This goes for everything from height, to IQ, and to the quality of professionals, accountants included.

Normal Curve
Standard Deviation

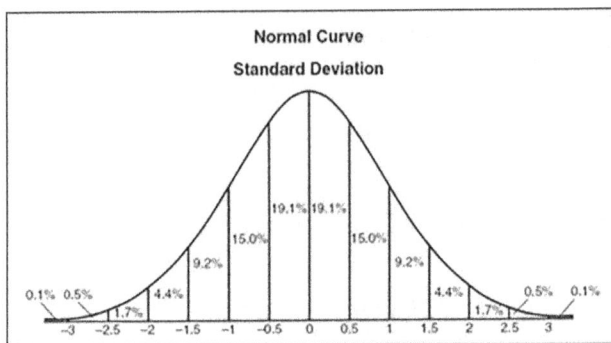

This figure demonstrates normal distribution. For example, there's many people who are between five and six foot, but very few under five foot or over six foot five inches. In layman's terms, the vast majority of people are average whilst a few are exceptional at either extreme.

As a businessperson, there's every chance your dealings with exceptionally good and exceptionally poor professionals have been rare, while most lie somewhere in between. Naturally you want to avoid the substandard and average and form strong relationships with leading accountants.

The best way to decide if an accountant is one that excels or otherwise, is whether or not you can consider his fees as an investment rather than a cost.

This report tells you how to ensure you're working with the best, and if you aren't, what you need to look for in your accountant. The information in this report will serve you in two major ways:

1. It will tell you the 7 Biggest Mistakes you can make with your accountant, and
2. By knowing the 7 Biggest Mistakes, it'll put you in a position to find a premium accountant who's an ideal fit for your business if your current one is lacking.

Working with the Wrong Accountant Means Throwing $$$ Away

As you know, business, small business in particular, is incredibly competitive. In the race to the finish line, you simply can't afford the added burden of an average or poor accountant. It literally can be the difference between winning and losing, business failure or success.

When I speak to small business owners there's a few issues nearly always mentioned:

- There's the competition breathing down their neck.
- The vast amount of energy they put into their business.
- The lack of service they receive from their accountants, and how much they pay for their services.

Let me provide you with an example. When I was in practice, I was approached by a business owner we'll call Paul. Another client had referred him. Paul was in a great deal of distress as he was losing money monthly in a business renowned for being a reasonably safe bet. His accountant told him it was all over. His advice was that he should call it quits and sell his business for whatever he could get.

The business was a well-located petrol station with all the handy corner shop offerings people so often buy on the run. For it to lose money something had to be seriously wrong.

I looked at the profitability of the business and dissected the results into the various product lines. We discovered the business was actually selling a particular product at less than its cost, creating a significant loss. It turned out the night manager had made an underhand deal with the deliveryman for this particular product. He was paying him for stock that never hit the shelves, and they divided the ill-gotten gains between them.

Paul turned the business around and sold it for a hefty profit. Paul is now a very successful businessman having moved on to bigger and better things. With our assistance, he learnt two crucial business rules. Not all employees are created equal. And the same goes for accountants.

The Vast Majority of Accountants Like to do a Good Job, but the Best Commit to Professional Excellence

There's every chance you're used to dealing with average-to-good accountants. They do what you ask them. They mostly do it on time. They mostly do a decent job. But in order for your business to reach its potential, that's simply not good enough.

Your stock standard accountant has the mindset of an order taker. By this I mean they simply do what they're asked without adding value, without offering professional insight, and without assisting your business to grow.

Basically, they're simply acting like a bookkeeper who's got a handle on MYOB, whilst charging you as if they were a professional accountant immersed in assisting you achieve your business goals. For their competent indifference, you get a hefty bill ranging from $150 to $400 an hour, sometimes even more.

A poor or average accountant will simply crunch the numbers you give them, send you a substantial bill, and then you'll get a second bill from the ATO. It's a great deal for your accountant and taxman, but not so great for you.

In no way could this sort of transaction be considered an investment. It's a task easily performed by a competent bookkeeper or yourself with the right software. The way small business owners are treated by the majority of accountants is disappointing. The poor and the average accountants bring down the reputation of proactive and service-minded professionals. However, it's a hard truth my profession needs to face up to. Just like the fact 90% of the work performed is number crunching.

I'll also make another less than flattering observation about my profession. When dealing with your accountant you've most likely come across someone who is very fee conscious, to the point where they've put you off asking the questions that need to be asked. It shouldn't—and needn't be this way. With the right accountant it isn't.

With the Help of an Expert, Proactive Accountant Your Investment in their Fees will Pay for Itself Many Times Over.

Being a rare breed, proactive accountants are hard to find. So how do you spot one?

It's a combination of their approach to service, their knowledge, and attitude. Proactive accountants look and behave differently. They're so much more than simple number crunchers. They…

- Take the time to understand your business and personal situation.
- Are friendly and service orientated.
- Offer ideas, strategies and services aligned with your goals.
- Do not charge you for phone calls, emails and quick meetings.
- 'Check in' regularly to see how you're going—at no charge.
- Price your work in advance so you have no surprise bills.
- Build enduring professional relationships with you.
- Ask for your opinion on how they can serve you better.
- Are focused on a quick turnaround time of your work.
- Advise you well in advance of forthcoming tax bills so there are no surprises.
- They speak in your language—no confusing jargon—and do not 'beat around the bush' when they tell you what you need to do.
- Offer a range of business improvement, wealth creation and asset protection services.

'How can I find an accountant like this?' I hear you ask. Allow me to show you…

Take a few moments to settle in and relax, as you discover how to engage the accountant who's an ideal fit for your business in terms of expertise, attitude and fees.

Discover the 7 Biggest Mistakes Small Business Owners Make with Their Accountants.

As we've said, there's a huge difference in the quality of accountants, from the motivated, proactive and service orientated, to the dud who has barely mastered a calculator and little more.

These following mistakes bring your attention to what is right and wrong with your relationship with your current accountant. After you've read it through ask yourself the questions:

1. Are you getting value for money?
2. Is this accountant good for my business?
3. Which of these 7 mistakes am I making?

If you are making any of the 7 Biggest Mistakes, it's important not to blame yourself. Any accountant interested in your continuing business success and growth will ensure you avoid these mistakes as a matter of course. The onus is on them.

Biggest Mistake #1: Not Asking For A Fixed Price

Too many accountants operate on the basis of you having an 'open cheque book.' They'll do the job and get you to pay it without a fixed price quote.

If you have a an average or worse accountant there's a chance they'll throw in computer breakdowns, or the amount of time it might take a less expert junior accountant to get the job done. These sub-par accountants are basically being paid for their own inefficiencies and cost-cutting measures when they send you a bill determined on their hourly rate. Simply do not do business with accountants of this type.

Imagine if your mechanic came to you after he'd repaired

your car, and said, 'It took me twice as long because I had to wait for a part to come in, so I'm going to have to double your bill.' That's what you can expect from low-end accountants.

On the other hand, skilled accountants are willing to offer a fixed price. They've factored in both problems and periods of exceptional productivity. They know their own capacities, and they know how long a job will take once they discuss it with you. They do an excellent job and they charge reasonable fees.

Therefore demand a fixed price. Any accountant worth their salt will be happy to offer a fixed price. They're confident in their ability to deliver. Knowing what your fees are will ensure you aren't slugged with any nasty surprises. Accountants have been in the game for years if not decades; they know what your job is worth.

Biggest Mistake #2: You Don't Get the Advice You Need

I see this all the time: *business owners being more confused at the end of a meeting with their accountant than at the beginning.*

You pay your accountants for advice—not for them to give you a headache with impenetrable jargon and more options than you can keep track of. If you have a problem that needs fixing, or a strategy you're unsure of, you need solid advice from your accountant. That's their job.

If they can't give you a 'yes' or 'no' answer, they need to be able to give you the pros and cons of the situation. If the matter is particularly delicate, your accountant should at least be able to say, 'If it was my decision, I would do this, but you must realise this is a very delicate matter and who knows what the other party will do,' or similar.

If they can't or won't do this because they lack insight, knowledge and confidence, it's time to let them go. Right now.

Biggest Mistake #3: You Use Your Accountant as an Over-qualified Bookkeeper or Tax Agent.

Don't let your accountant be a bookkeeper. Bookkeepers charge $50 an hour. Accountants charge up to ten times that amount.

Accountants have an obligation to their clients to give advice, aside from controlling bookkeeping and completing tax returns. Sub-par and average accountants prepare financial statements and simply post the final results and tax returns to the client. There's no analysis of the results, or suggestions to grow the business or deal with issues that have arisen.

Without having to be asked, the right accountant will offer their expert analysis on:

1. Your actual results.
2. Ways to limit your tax bill.
3. The efficiencies of your operations compared to your expectations, market trends or benchmarks.
4. The effect your results have on the asset value of your business and your ability to enjoy your future as you see it.
5. Any and all outstanding issues a quality accountant will notice. The right accountant will pick up what others, including yourself, miss.

If your accountant is giving you the advice outlined above, you're one of the lucky few. You don't want your accountant to simply compile your results. That's a job for bookkeepers. You get value out of your accountant when they implement their cumulative knowledge, ensuring the ATO get as little of your money as possible.

It's at this time the 'right' accountant will offer you their analysis on the areas we've just run through. If not, you'd be wise to go to another accountant promptly.

Biggest Mistake #4: You Don't Ask For Guarantees

When dealing with your accountant guarantees are invaluable. An excellent accountant will offer them to you without prompting.

There are three areas you must cover with a guarantee:

1. The time frame for any work performed.
2. How quickly any of your communications (phone, email, etc.) will be responded to.
3. How often the two of you meet and how long those meetings go for.

Even an average accountant will be able to guarantee all of the above. The best of accountants will reimburse you when these guarantees are broken. If your accountant doesn't offer you a guarantee you can be certain your business success and customer satisfaction are not their top priority. *It's time to move on.*

Biggest Mistake #5: You Expect Your Accountant to 'Have Your Back' When There is No Relationship

For most small business owners, there are only two times they visit their accountant: at tax time or when they're in crisis.

To develop a fruitful relationship with your accountant,

it's crucial you view them as more than someone to do your tax return or help you in crisis management. Excellent accountants are experts in managing a business crisis, *but if you have the right relationship you'll be much less likely to get into a crisis in the first place.* If you keep one of those exceptional accountants updated they'll help you recognise and navigate around any icebergs on your course to business success.

Just like a personal trainer or a doctor, an accountant will keep you on track, advise on technique and provide ideas if they know what's going on. This means seeing them more than once a year or when things are looking grim.

If you have a strong business relationship with the right accountant they will…

- Raise and highlight with you issues they can help you with—just like doctors they will have specialties.
- If you make an investment without their knowledge, quickly advise you of the 'what ifs' of your actions and give remedies to correct any problems you may have created.

Ideally you should see your accountant every two months, and I would suggest three times a year at minimum. The more a proactive accountant knows about your business the more they can help.

Building an ongoing professional relationship is a sure way to keep your accountant engaged in your work—to keep you at the front of their mind. Making it social will take it to the next level. If you invite them to social events, invariably you will discuss business and get some free advice. Don't expect it, or take it for granted, but it's one way for you to turn that lunchtime meeting or a chat over drinks into a great investment. The more well considered you are by your accountant the more likely they'll think of you when opportunities present.

Make certain you've got *at least* one meeting with your accountant booked in advance, if not the entire years. This ensures you consider each other in the long-term, and proves to your accountant you're in it for the long haul.

It's a small thing, but make sure your accountant has your up to date details so they can get back to you without undue delay.

Biggest Mistake #6: You Don't Communicate Your Short, Medium and Long-term Business Goals

Tell your accountant about your short, medium and long-term business goals. Quality accountants often have a pretty good idea of what they might be whatever the case. However, when you give your accountant a detailed vision of your goals they're in a much better position to assist business growth.

Providing them with a detailed account of your short, medium and long-term goals will allow them to:

- Help you discern any problems you may not be aware of
- Provide you with expert knowledge and advice.
- Understand where you are headed so they can inform you of any developments related to your business.
- They will see you're serious about your future. The more seriously you take yourself, the more seriously they'll take you.

If you just tell your accountant what to do without giving them any context it's an invitation for them to act like *simple order-takers.* It holds back a good accountant from giving you appropriate advice, minimising their ability to put their expertise at the service of your business.

Here's an example:

Many small businesses instruct their accountants to set them up under a 'company structure'. A top-tier accountant with an understanding of your business can readily discern if this is a wise choice or not. An average or weak accountant will simply take the order and set up the company structure even though this may be a poor choice and damage the business.

If you see your accountant regularly over a period of time a solid bond of trust will build. If it doesn't, you're better off moving onto to someone you can trust.

Biggest Mistake #7: You Expect the Principal to Do All the Work

Many small businesses feel it's important the principal or partner in the accounting firm does their work. They can feel like a second-class client if this isn't the case.

If you have a great accountant, your worry is unfounded. Senior accountants of quality are experts in directing their staff. In fact, quality seniors inevitably lead quality staff. Juniors often go the extra mile as part of their professional development and to repay the trust placed in them.

It's like going to a large and reputable mechanic. Chances are several different technicians will work on your car, and the 'boss' probably won't touch it. All the while they oversee staff and contribute when necessary,—as well as carrying the responsibility of the business.

One of the best bits of advice I can give is to meet the team working with you. If you can't meet them in person, organise a Skype conference. At the very least speak to them on the phone.

Take Some Time to Think About Your Own Situation...

So please give yourself a minute or two to review my advice and ask yourself how your accountant fares.

Here's a summary to help you:

- Biggest Mistake #1: You Don't Ask for a Fixed Price.
- Biggest Mistake #2: You Don't Get the Advice You Need.
- Biggest Mistake #3: You Use Your Accountant as an Over-qualified Bookkeeper or Tax Agent.
- Biggest Mistake #4: You Don't Ask for Guarantees.
- Biggest Mistake #5: You Expect your Accountant to 'Have Your Back' When There is no Relationship.
- Biggest Mistake #6: You Don't Communicate Your Short, Medium and Long-Term Business Goals.
- Biggest Mistake #7: You Expect the Principal to Do All the Work.

What to do Next?

So, you've had some time to ask yourself the questions that need asking and assess how effectively your accountant works for your business. If you are one of the very few who can say they have a near perfect accountant, you're lucky indeed. My colleagues and I guess around 9-10% of small businesspeople are as fortunate as you.

If you're not one of the very fortunate few, we'd like to invite you to talk to us about any questions or concerns you may have about dealing with accountants and finding the ideal accountant to get your business booming. That's why we've set aside some time to offer a rare business opportunity for the first twenty-five people who get in touch this month only.

We're offering small businesses a complimentary, no obligation consultation (valued at $397... including an unbeaten 200% guarantee, but more on that shortly).

It will give you the opportunity to discuss any questions inspired by this report. You will be able to talk to me, Geoff Richmond about your business issues. I'll be able to share insider secrets on what will make your business more profitable only a handful of accountants know about, but certainly don't share for free.

We'll give you all the information you need to know about turning your accountancy fees into an investment rather than a cost. During our time together you'll...

- Acquire the knowledge you need so you can get the best out of your accountant by asking all the right questions.
- Explore your business vision—how your business works and what you need to know and do to achieve your business goals.
- Discover opportunities for you to investigate with your accountant.
- Eliminate time, energy and money wasting financial services, bookkeeping and business advice.

- Resolve any doubts in your mind about your business direction.

It's undeniably an attractive opportunity, even more so because it costs nothing...

As a small businessperson you're probably thinking, 'There's no such thing as a free lunch. What's the catch?'

And it's a wise question to ask. Let me explain.

In South Australia, we estimate *just 1 in 10 accountancy firms are proactive*. That's not many, so we figure, we can either get you working effectively with your own accountant, or if you decide after our conversation you need to change accountants we can help you find the right one.

We're offering an innovative solution to the many issues small business owners have with their accountants.

We're Best Understood as an Accountancy Broker.

We help proactive accountants find business owners serious about success. Conversely, we help business owners find the best possible proactive accountant that's going to help them grow their business—to assist in their business dreams becoming realised.

Just like an insurance broker finds the best insurance for their clients, we do the same for businesspeople looking for the ideal accountant.

Our service comes at *no cost to you*, so I'll just quickly explain how it works. As an accountancy broker we:

- Help you determine an appropriate fee you can take to the accountant.
- Discern the appropriate guarantees you need.
- Find the right accountant at the right price with

the right guarantees. Negotiate with the accountant if the fee is not immediately accepted.

- Serve you as both an intermediary and an advocate in your ongoing relationship with the accountant.
- If the accountant proves to be the wrong one for the client, a better match will be found at no cost.
- Provide business-consulting services on top of accountant brokerage.
- Provide ongoing phone consultancy without the clock running.

'How Does it Work Out that I Pay Nothing?'

As an accountancy broker we match you with your ideal accounts professional. *You pay no fee* because the accountant pays us 20% of their fee in the first year and 10% of their fee every year thereafter, whilst you pay the accountant's normal fee. This means *you pay nothing for our services,* and it's in our best interest to find you the ideal accountant as your satisfaction means ongoing revenue for us.

Our TWICE YOUR HOURLY RATE 200% Money Back Guarantee!

We promise to give you the individual attention and expert assistance your business deserves. And we back up that promise with an unheard of *200% guarantee.* We're so confident we can assist you in getting your business where you want it to be,—in helping you rake in the profits we're willing to offer a unique guarantee.

If you aren't completely satisfied with the complimentary expert assistance we provide, we will pay you at TWICE YOUR HOURLY RATE.

Incredible as it may seem, we will reimburse you twice your usual hourly rate if you feel your time has been wasted.

So please call us right now on +61 (08) 8239 0122 to speak to one of our friendly staff and schedule your complimentary appointment. You've got nothing to lose and everything to gain.

This is your opportunity to get the expert advice you deserve and to get the support you need for your business to boom. So call us now on +61 (08) 8239 0122. We only have space for the first twenty-five people who get in touch this month only so please don't delay.

But before I finish up I just thought I'd pass on some food for thought.

The world's leading publisher of accountancy material recently released a survey. They discovered accountants spend 63% of the time performing basic bookkeeping tasks, while being paid like an accountant of course. They also discovered 21% of businesses fail due to poor professional advice, while 26% go under simply because they didn't seek any advice at all.

So, for future business success and personal prosperity please call now on +61 (08) 8239 0122, it's completely risk and obligation free. I look forward to assisting you in growing your business.

Regards,

Geoff Richmond,

Chartered Accountant, Business Owner and Professional Accountancy Broker.

Happy 29th February!

Appendix S

Standards Not Met Offer

As you know, 2IC Management recently changed to Value Pricing Agreements (VPAs) with our clients for any work we perform.

We have set performance standards for 2IC Management which we promise to meet as part of the agreement. If our services do not provide you with any value we also offer a money back guarantee.

As well as encouraging clients to give us their feedback on our performance, we also assess our own performance. If we feel we have not met our standards then we are proactive in acknowledging this and taking the necessary action to ensure that we meet these standards in the future.

We believe we have not met our standards for [insert reason here]. However, rather than offer a cash refund to you we thought the attached invitation would give you value of a different kind.

We value our relationship with you and look forward to many years of mutual success.

The team at 2IC Management invites

[CLIENT]

To dine as our guests at

Urban Bistro, 160 Fullarton Road, Rose Park

Please contact Sally Davey, Restaurant Manager,
on 8331 2400 to make a booking

Authorised by
2IC Management

Not redeemable for cash, redemption value at the
discretion of 2IC Management Pty Ltd

Expires [enter 6 months from today's date]